The

Origins

of

School Violence

The

Origins

of

School Violence

Sean M. Brooks, Ph.D.

Foreword by Douglas M. Brooks, Ph.D.

ISBN-10: 1791944388
ISBN-13: 978-1791944384

Kindle Direct Publishing

Printed in the United States of America

Acknowledgements: Thank you to Dr. Jennifer Courduff, Dr. Heather Pederson, Dr. Narjis Hyder and Dr. Wade Smith for their editorial work of the original manuscript. Finally, thank you to my family for their support and dedication to teacher education.

TABLE OF CONTENTS

For Douglas and Barbara

That which is not good for the beehive cannot be good for the bees.

-Marcus Aurelius

FOREWORD

School should be the safest place in a student's life. The faculty and staff assigned to a school should know that a student who feels threated and afraid—does not learn. Students worry. They wake up with the same fears that sleep helped them escape, if they slept. Only the cause of that fear is now back. Students imagine what will happen, until it happens. This worry interferes with every-thing. Then it happens again. It's a push, a shove, a hurtful name, an exclusion, being picked last or unfairly singled out, a classroom embarrassment, a game never won, a threat on the way home, a ride on a bus with tormentors, or a mean text message or slander-ous social media post.

Schools are inundated with daily rhythms, routines and hab-its. Students can't escape them, and they not only feel trapped—they are trapped. Another threatening or humiliating episode with a student or a teacher is now over. It will be a whole day before it happens again. But, the escape is futile, unless someone does something. That somebody should be a classroom teacher or ad-ministrator. Too often, it is not.

Dr. Sean Brooks has painstakingly researched a gaping hole in teacher preparation and in-service training. This hole is shameful and one that teacher educators and school administrators should be rushing to fill. His three main questions were straightforward: (a) What training did you receive in your pre-service programs on the causes of conflict and violence in school, conflict resolution and violence prevention, (b) as a current educator and administrator, what episodes of conflict and violence are you experiencing here at school, and (c) what in-service training have you received on the causes of conflict and violence in school, conflict resolution and violence prevention?" His research setting was an urban school district that was roughly 74 percent Caucasian.

I am certain that the teachers and administrators in his sample told him the truth. Educators tend to tell the truth when they are asked serious questions in private. While his research process utilized a case-study methodology, its easily phenomenological. He listened. He probed. He recorded. He analyzed. Finally, he reported his conclusions in this work. Dr. Brooks demonstrates that Colleges of Education and K-12 school districts are not responding with any urgency.

You can read the work. It is thoughtful and focused on a matter that will only get worse before it gets better. Violent acts in school settings have reached the shores of America's classrooms like a Tsunami. Generations of students are now exposed to every form of violence. Systemic curriculum improvements need to be made at the pre-service level. Fully integrated education needs to exist within every school. "Lockdowns" are a reaction. Prevention is what is needed.

These changes will come slowly for two reasons. Pre-service curriculum changes exist at a glacial pace, and occasional in-service guest speakers are predictably ineffective or make matters worse. University courses are still driven by ancient disciplines. Content is selected at the whim of professors who are far removed from schools. There is no undergraduate or graduate education course titled, "School Violence and Conflict Resolution." At best, exposure is a unit in a course far removed from student teaching and the entry year. Currently, many of the professors in teacher education programs are more concerned with "social justice," rather than the justice they should be serving. This justice involves teacher preparation that can keep prospective teachers, school staff and students safe, healthy and free from violence within school-based environments.

Dr. Sean Brooks' research has put the next buoy in the river. This marker should guide the slowly turning barges of teacher preparation programs and in-service experiences. Someone with vision, insight, commitment, quality research, and the personal experience that drives them to move ahead of the crowd—often place these markers.

These researchers often travel alone. They imagine the next danger before others see it. They measure the danger. They leave their mark and move upriver to the next danger. School violence and the absence of training offered in teacher education is the looming danger.

—Douglas M. Brooks, Ph.D.
Full Professor of Teacher Education
Miami University

PREFACE

As a youth, a second child and a natural observer, I began to easily recognize the presence of violent behavior within school-based environments. With each observable moment, I would look to see which adult was acting appropriately to manage such behaviors. What I witnessed, more often than not, was inconsistency at best and demonstrative negligence at it's worst.

I was appalled at the implementation and approval of the very dogmas that generated division among school-aged students, and the willful participation by the very adults who were charged with teaching and protecting them. I soon realized that humans, of all ages, were responsible for violence in school—not just students themselves.

As I aged and traveled throughout middle school and high school, the observable behaviors became worse, while educators and administrators themselves were the primary provocateurs. The punishments that followed for such behaviors were clearly not making a dent. Too often, students would engage in verbal and physical altercations with little to no adult interventions ever taking place. For example, during one episode in high school, it was well known among the student population on this particular day, that a physical fight was going to occur outside of the school, across the street. As word spread around the school, not a single adult acted on the widespread student conversations that detailed the organized confrontation. Adults either didn't know or they willfully ignored these verbal student exchanges.

The result led to an enormous pre-fight group-circle of over 100 students. Two football players, both of whom were on the same team, fought one another. One garnished a pair of brass knuckles and proceeded to almost beat the other half to death. At no point did teachers or administrators preventively intervene. The entire incident took place without adult involvement. (If you thought, even for a moment, that both football players were minorities, you would be wrong. Both football players were Caucasian, as were all of the male and female onlookers—stretching from the most "popular" students to the least "popular").

Sadly, when many novices (adults and youth) think of school violence, they think of race, class or socioeconomic location as a determining factor. Violence in school is not a matter of skin color, accidental-societal class or location. The integumentary system and skin color are physiologically incapable of making decisions. Therefore, violence and its predecessors exist within any school environment or any environment for that matter, regardless of socioeconomic surroundings, demographics, income, race, class, gender, age or ethnicity. Violence is a human behavior. Violence in school is a human-being problem. This highlights two simple rhetorical questions—who makes school related policy? Is it students and their families, or adults who work inside and around the American educational system?

When I became an education major in undergraduate school, I witnessed not just an abundance of obliviousness toward the subject of violence in school, but I witnessed the complete absence of a conversation ever taking place within a classroom setting. I was wishing such a conversation and formal education would be present at this level of preparatory "higher" education. I was sorely mistaken.

I stopped wishing and I investigated this subject on my own. I did so by taking unrequired sociology courses and reading about political science, economics, history, psychology and adolescent development, on my own time—all while reading about historic and current educational philosophy. I also read my own curriculum of secondary-level health education and recognized that the subjects of conflict and violence were going to be a part of my required teaching.

Upon teaching, I witnessed other health educators in middle schools and high schools ignore the subjects of conflict and violence in the required textbooks. They instead relied heavily on the physical education aspects of the curriculum, which were and are insignificant in my opinion (i.e., competition, game playing, learning the rules of volleyball, taking your cloths off in front of your peers for a grade [i.e., dressing out in locker rooms without proper supervision,] running a timed mile, how much can you bench-press? etc.). I also witnessed the same absence of teaching regarding the required subjects of dating violence, drug use, suicidal behavior, mental and emotional disorders and other critical topics that were impacting both school-aged students and society as a whole.

The common excuse I heard repeatedly from other health educators was, "Well, we don't get to those subjects because we don't have enough time." This was, and is code-talk for; "We don't know about these subjects and we don't care about them, so we don't teach them. We spend more time on the subjects we like and the ones we know." It just so happens; such a response is psychologically referred to as moral justification and moral disengagement. So what they really mean is, "We don't know what we don't know—and then we make quick excuses for not knowing, thereby justifying our noninvolvement because we don't want to learn something new."

The same responses are now given within undergraduate and graduate institutions. If teacher education students, regardless of the subjects they intend to teach, are not receiving a formal education on the antecedents to conflict and violence in school from their teacher-education professors, then one could infer that they're being set up to fail. One can educate another about a serious subject without creating a culture of uncertainty and frustration, both of which may ultimately lead to career discouragement and career abandonment. However, this subject, its causes and preventive measures must be known first before anyone can teach them to another.

Pre-service teachers are entering undergraduate institutions with an expectation that they will be taught by passionate, optimistic educators who will prepare them for the realities of being a teacher in today's world. Sadly, an epidemic of anger, political ideology and curricular distraction can easily infiltrate preparatory instruction. This can easily corrode the individual classroom-instructional approaches of professors, many of which may simply lack knowledge regarding their own subject matter, in particular through a lens of today's school-level violence. An easy example of this lack of knowledge occurs almost every time a violent act takes place within a school-based environment. If you ever hear someone arbitrarily mention a school shooting, they fail to understand what leads to such an event. If someone uses the dismissive phrase "loner" to describe a student, or that school shooters are always "loners," this too shows a collective lack of understanding. In short, when buzzwords are used and repeated like a bird call, in particular across the mainstream media, true knowledge on the subject, and its causes, are absent.

Receiving a comprehensive education on the antecedents to conflict and violence in school is now a professional necessity. Pre-service teachers need to be taught educational philosophy in the right order, beginning with an accurate history—that brings us directly to the modern day, while not abandoning proven historic fact. Ultimately, educators need to be taught to succeed, not taught to fail.

I recommend making this text a reference for your future investigations and experiences. I also recommend reading this book more than twice if you are in the educational field, and if you're not interested in perpetuating the problem or you're not profiting from the existence of the problem. As this book will describe, the presence of violence in school is a matter of *adult* efficacy and perhaps the purposeful implementation of unworkable policies by the very adults who claim to keep students and staff safe.

Answers will never show themselves in the form of a "school-based violence-prevention program." Answers will only show themselves through the investigative approach of reading facts and connecting the dots. Moreover, as research-based investigations show, the most ethical teachers and administrators within school-based environments both want and need a comprehensive, objective education at all levels of their professional maturation; early, accurately and before it's too late.

Chapter 1

Background and Introduction

Pre-service and in-service education for teachers and administrators can vary between institutions. Some formal education programs train teachers for curriculum development, leadership characteristics, lesson planning, and subject-based knowledge acquisition (Bauman & Del Rio, 2006). However, some pre-service teacher education institutions and in-service professional development programs may not formally address the antecedents to conflict and violence within school environments (Bauman & Del Rio, 2006). Within the United States, rates of teenage violence (ages 13-19 years) exceed other developed countries (David-Ferdon & Simon, 2014). Many manifestations of conflict and violence both exist and lead to youth substance abuse, lowered academic achievement, mental illness, suicidal ideation, and social distrust (Bushman et al., 2016). Examining the perceptions educators have regarding school violence prevention is needed (Bushman et al., 2016).

Pre-service teachers report fears of anxiety relating to their evaluation of students, the ability to control students, managing a classroom setting, and evaluation by supervisors (Matoti & Lekhu, 2016). Pre-service teachers also possess varying perceptions of the definition of violence, including knowledge of the various forms it can take within school settings (Özabaci, & Erkan, 2015). Differing perceptions on school-level violence call for further education to deter such acts (Hertzog, Harpel, & Rowley, 2016). The ability of students to problem solve and resolve conflicts may ultimately be mitigated by the teacher's level of education on such issues (Turkum, 2011). Given these challenges, pre-service undergraduate teacher-education institutions and current in-service professional development programs could address the teenage health-related factors that lead to conflict and violence in school.

The extent to which pre-service and in-service programs have addressed teenage health-related antecedents to conflict and violence remains in question. Teenage students continue to be exposed to health-related issues that involve bullying, cyber-bullying, substance abuse, dating violence, depression, and suicidal thought. An educator's experience, personal efficacy, and their understanding of the levels of strain that lead to such issues are essential. Furthermore, an educator's pre-service and in-service training may have a direct correlation to an educator's willingness to understand and teach both students and fellow staff members about conflict resolution and violence prevention.

The sections throughout this chapter include the varying perceptions of education regarding the existence of conflict and violence within school-based environments. I discuss the perceptions of the existence of school-based and health-based factors that may underwrite its existence. Overall, I examined teacher and administrator perceptions of their previous education and the existence of conflict and violence within school settings to better understand pre-service teacher training and in-service professional development.

A formal exposure to conflict and violence-related education might influence self-efficacy. As perceptions of violence in school and methods for prevention vary (Espelage, Polanin, & Low, 2014; Richard, Schneider, & Mallet, 2012), teachers' perceptions of bullying and harassment among students within school environments differ from educator to educator (Charmaraman, Jones, Stein, & Espelage, 2013; Espelage et al., 2014). Teachers also report that their professional development experiences are not addressing these topics (Charmaraman et al., 2013; Espelage et al., 2014).

Students may report more incidents of violent behavior in school than their teachers. For example, Gome-Garibello, Sayka, Moore, and Talwar (2013) argued that the ability of teachers to recognize lying among students who were bullied varied. Age is not a determining factor when accurately or confidently assessing a student's honesty (Gome-Garibello et al., 2013). Moreover, pre-service teacher candidates also report less assurance involving families with the school environment and school communications within school-based settings (i.e., family involvement, classroom management, content knowledge, planning for instruction and professionalism) (Lee, Tice, Collins, Brown, Smith, & Fox, 2012).

With many conflict and violence prevention strategies existing within school systems, peer mentoring is accepted as a necessary restorative approach (Peurača & Vejmelka, 2015). As students grow up and separate from their parents, they tend to adopt more peer-driven relationships and interactions (Peurača & Vejmelka, 2015). Peer-mediation as a preventive measure can promote positive communication that increases positive relationships, while decreasing school related violence among students and staff (Peurača

& Vejmelka, 2015). However, school-wide attempts to reduce bullying through anti-bullying programs largely fail to have a lasting presence within schools and among staff members (Richard, Schneider, & Mallet, 2012). Poor school climate, security, and student-to-teacher relationships tend to be the largest predictors of violence and bullying behaviors within school environments (Richard, Schneider, & Mallet, 2012).

Numerous health-related factors contribute to the existence of conflict and violence in school such as: (a) bullying, (b) cyber bullying, (c) teenage dating violence, (d) teenage substance abuse, and (e) teenage depression and suicidal thought. The levels of exposure educators receive to these health-related factors could be understood. The presence of these contributors within pre-service training programs and in-service professional development could be explored. In the problem statement, I underscore the relevant gaps regarding the presence of conflict and violence preventive education and address the varying perceptions. This case study intended to address a gap in the research regarding the presence of conflict resolution and violence prevention within pre-service and in-service teacher education.

The Centers for Disease Control and Prevention (CDC, 2015) within the 2015 National Youth Risk Behavior Survey (YRBS), defined violence as "the intentional use of physical force or power, against another person, group, or community, with the behavior likely to cause physical or psychological harm" (p.1). Ribeiro, Ribeiro, Pratesi, and Gandolfi (2015) reported that physical, psychological, and sexual violence are most commonly reported among middle and high school students aged 13-19 years. Teachers' perceptions of school related violence might vary based on the previous education and experiences (Charmaraman, Jones, Stein, & Espelage, 2013). Professional development for school violence prevention may also be lacking depending on the previous and current expertise of administrators (Charmaraman et al., 2013). Furthermore, the presence of conflict resolution education is minimal across numerous courses of study within college level instruction for graduate and undergraduate students (Zelizer, 2015). A lack of conflict resolution instruction may also contribute to conflicts within workplaces (Zelizer, 2015).

Espelage et al. (2013) stated that students experience many different forms of violence within school environments. Students are not alone, as teachers can also be the victims of violence from either students or other coworkers (Espelage et al., 2013). Bradshaw, Waasdorp, O'Brennan, and Gulemetova (2013) argued that teachers need further training regarding health-related issues such as; sexual orientation, gender issues, racial issues, and mental and emotional conditions.

A gap existed in the research regarding an examination of a multitude of geographically diverse pre-service teacher education institutions. This gap also stretched out to encompass the experiences of these educators when they themselves were undergraduates and their levels of preparation regarding conflict resolution and violence prevention before becoming formal teachers/administrators. The innovation lies in the understanding of a presence or absence of preventive education based on educator's geographically diverse pre-service teacher education experiences. This shed light on the existence and quality of conflict and violence preventative education for prospective educators. This study contributed to a body of knowledge by obtaining educators' perspectives of their previous and current education within their pre-service and in-service levels of teacher education.

The purpose of this case study was to understand urban high school educators' perceptions and experiences with conflict resolution and violence prevention within their pre-service and in-service education. Understanding the perceptions of educators based on their geographically diverse teacher-education institutions addressed a gap in the research regarding the presence of conflict resolution and violence prevention education for pre-service teachers. Data analysis relied on audio-recorded interviews and a follow-up focus group that sought to understand the perceptions and experiences of educators relating to their pre-service education, current experiences with student health-related antecedents to violent behavior, and in-service training.

Three questions were addressed throughout this exploration. (a) What are the perceptions of urban high school teachers and administrators pre-service education relating to conflict resolution and violence prevention? (b) What are the current experiences of urban high school teachers and administrators regarding student-related conflict and violence in school? (c) How do urban high school teachers and administrators perceive the effects of in-service conflict resolution and violence prevention education?

The theoretical approach to this exploration was comprised of three theories: constructivism, self-efficacy theory (SET), and general strain theory (GST). The quality of personal and educational experiences while generating meaning, specifically within educational environments, is the basis for the theory of constructivism (Dewey, 1938). Constructivist theory is defined when one builds on their past and present experiences to form new understanding, specifically in this case within the field of acquired pre-service and in-service teacher education. As experiences can be both educational and yet counterproductive, the quality of experience and education may be at risk (Dewey, 1938). The responsibility of the educator is to drive the formal learning and experiential learning of their students (Dewey, 1938). Furthermore, the quality of such education and shared experiences may be contingent on the worth of the educator's history (Dewey, 1938). Based on the theory of constructivism, teachers apply meaning among their pupils through experience and formal education by connecting the school environments to the outside world (Dewey, 1938). (*A side note: I disagree with John Dewey on practically everything. He was an agnostic-socialist, a Marxist and a humanist, and sadly he's considered the father of modern American education. His philosophies have systemically destroyed education in America. However, for the sole purpose of this study, I used the theory of Constructivism (which he simply expanded on from the original theory) to simply state that experiences that match a formal education are more likely to ensure long-term knowledge within an individual. For example, if a child reads a book about airplanes and then visits an airplane museum, that child is more likely to know more about airplanes than a child who only experiences one or the other by itself*).

SET states that when knowledge is not acquired, an individual's belief in their ability to achieve is diminished (Bandura, 1977). Furthermore, if an individual who possesses lowered self-belief in their abilities and holds an instructional position, the knowledge acquisition of those they instruction may suffer (Bandura, 1977). A failure to improve self-efficacy may lead to a moral justification regarding the absence of such knowledge (Bandura, 2016). In order to transfer messages in a purposeful way, the acquisition of information requires both formal education and experience (Bandura, 1977). Such exposure to quality information from knowledgeable instructors can formulate improved self-efficacy between both the instructor and the pupil (Bandura, 1977).

GST states that everyone is prone to frustration and aggression depending on the type and frequency of stressors (i.e., the inability to achieve positively valued goals; the removal of or threat to remove positively valued stimuli; to present a threat to one with noxious or negatively valued stimuli) (Agnew, 2001). Strain is likely to increase over time as one interacts with abundant stressors, thereby increasing the likelihood of delinquency and criminal behavior (Agnew, 2001). As many stressors impact frustration and aggression (i.e., failure to achieve goals, poverty, depression, anxiety, physical and sexual victimization), GST states that adults and youth are both susceptible to such stressors and the existence of short and long-term consequences (Agnew, 2006). An inability to receive accurate information or achieve goals may lead to episodes of strain, in particular in educational environments where there's an abundance of adults and youth (Agnew, 2006).

If educational programs for teachers fail to address the health-related factors that impact conflict and violence in school, constructivist approaches, self-efficacy, and knowledge of general strain may also be lacking.

The CDC 2015 YRBS reported the existence of 118 health-related factors that impact urban high school students. Understanding the past and current educational experiences and exposure teachers have specifically with (a) bullying, (b) cyber-bullying, (c) teenage dating violence, (d) teenage substance abuse, (e) teenage depression and suicidal thought, among their students (as highlighted in Chapter 2), may be dependent on the perceived quality of pre-service teacher education and current in-service education.

Within the designed study, I gathered the perceptions of urban high school teachers and administrators regarding their pre-service and in-service conflict resolution and violence prevention education. Educator's current perceptions of student-related conflict and violence in school were also obtained. Specifically, urban high school teachers and administrators were included in this process and purposefully selected. I attempted to elicit one core teacher per subject and grade (i.e., math, science, history, and literature; grades 10-12). Therefore, the two criteria for participation included: (a) the geographically diverse location of the participant's pre-service undergraduate teacher-education college or university; and (b) the subject and grade level the participating educator taught. An audio-recorded interview was conducted with each participant individually. I conducted an audio-recorded follow-up focus group of willing participants after the interview phase. The focus group primarily explored Research Questions 2 and 3. The focus group generated a dialogue among participants regarding student-related episodes of conflict and violence in school. The desired quality, quantity, and relevance of past, current and future in-service training for conflict resolution and violence prevention in school were discussed.

Case study methodology is utilized when one is examining the specific nature and characteristics of behaviors, managerial processes, relationships, and performances (Yin, 2009). This methodology addresses the need for understanding implementation processes, decision-making, and organizational change (Yin, 2009). Such an approach intends to examine and report on current ways of understating to facilitate future exploration of a highlighted element (Stake, 1978). Ultimately, case study methodology may leave those who are investigated with more focus, thereby enhancing humanistic experiences and furthering understanding within a specific environment (Stake, 1978).

Below are common words and phrases that are used throughout this text. Their definitions are as follows:

Conflict: Although there are no absolute definitions of conflict, Nicholson (1992) described conflict as an activity that takes place when conscious beings (individuals or groups) wish to carry out mutually inconsistent acts concerning their wants, needs, or obligations.

Conflict resolution: Forsyth (2009) described conflict resolution as the methods and processes involved in facilitating a peaceful ending of conflict and retribution where committed group members attempt to resolve conflicts through communication of differing viewpoints, which require negotiation.

Educator: An educator is defined within this study as an individual who possesses the responsibility of teaching another, or provides instruction or education (i.e., college or university professor, urban high school teacher, school-level administrator) (Cochran-Smith, 2006).

In-service: In-service refers to the training or professional development typically received by educators who hold current teaching or administrative positions (Indoshi, 2003).

Interpersonal violence: According to Dahlberg and Krug (2002), interpersonal violence is described as the intentional use of physical force or power, threatened or actual, against an individual, group, or community that results in or has a high likelihood of resulting in injury, death, psychological harm, mal-development, or deprivation.

Pre-service: Pre-service refers to the title given to an undergraduate within a teacher-training program at the college or university level, before becoming a formal teacher (Van Nuland, 2011).

Violence prevention: Violence prevention refers to the measures taken to prevent or reduce those acts defined as violent (World Health Organization [WHO], 2017).

Keep in mind that most school-based conflict resolution or violence prevention programs only present themselves after an undesirable episode erupts within a school environment (Schultes, Stefanek, van de Schoot, Strohmeier, & Spiel, 2014). If such programs exist, only teachers with high responsiveness to such programs are likely to be successful with a dispersion of educational methods (Schultes et al., 2014). This is simply to say that some teachers who believe everything they are told from a superior are likely to implement such programs regardless of the program's legitimacy, while more competent educators examine the legitimacy of a program before any possible implementation. Additionally, such programs may fail to specifically examine targeted areas of concern that exist within a given school-based environment (Park-Higgerson, Perumean-Chaney, Bartolucci, Grimley, & Singh, 2008).

According to CDC (2015), urban high school youth are exposed to a multitude of factors that increase the chances of poor health that typically increase the chances of death. Moreover, another assumption involved teachers and administrators not expressing a need to explore this education given their specific course subject. However, I assumed the answers of each respondent accurately reflected their previous education, current experiences with conflict and violence in school, and their current perceptions of their educational training during the audio-recorded interview process. A final assumption was that I was able to accurately categorize meaning throughout the interview process and focus group while avoiding the insertion of my own values.

Within this study, I used a small population of teachers and administrators within an urban high school setting (12 teachers and two administrators). Urban high school teachers and administrators were also purposefully selected. I attempted to elicit one core teacher per subject and grade (i.e., math, science, history, and literature; grades 10-12). Therefore, the two criteria for participation included: (a) the geographically diverse location of the participant's pre-service undergraduate teacher-education college or university; and (b) the subject and grade level the participating educator taught.

This research study possessed multiple limitations. First, a limitation involved a smaller sampling of teachers (12) who teach core subjects (i.e., math, science, history, and literature). Secondly, an underpinning fear of honesty could have been present, as some educators may have feared workplace retribution for participation in a study regarding their current working environment. However, the current study aimed to address the quality, presence and frequency of such education for both teachers and administrators in an effort to improve the case-studied environment. Dispelling concerns to participants beforehand elicited honest responses. Such responses socially exposed a desire for change regarding pre-service education and in-service professional development that leads toward innovative curriculum.

The efficacy of administrators can have a dramatic impact on the efficacy of their fellow teachers (Mehdinezhad & Mansouri, 2016). It is possible that if educators believe a school environment is doing all they can to educate one another about a particular topic, this belief is largely driven by the beliefs of the school's administration (Mehdinezhad & Mansouri, 2016). Therefore, staff members disagreed with one another about the quality of in-service professional development, to some extent, which is typically delivered by administrators. Ultimately, the candidness of responses depended on the respondent's willingness to self-expose a lack of educational experiences related to conflict and violence prevention within pre-service and in-service teacher education. Fortunately this was not the case, as participants had no trepidation in self-disclosing their lack of knowledge on conflict resolution and violence prevention, nor their thoughts and true beliefs about the type and quality of their in-service training.

The literature on preparing teachers for conflict resolution and violence prevention in school is limited. While teacher education programs exist within colleges and universities, there is little literature on how all teachers are prepared for conflict resolution and violence prevention in school, and the antecedents that lead to such episodes. The results showed that pre-service and in-service education is not aligning itself with the current experiences of teachers and administrators regarding student-related episodes of conflict and violence. Consequently, current in-service professional development is not addressing conflict resolution and violence prevention in school for teachers and administrators. Any lack of education within this latter stage of professional development is primarily driven by the previous absence of conflict and violence prevention-based education within pre-service undergraduate and graduate teacher training. In-service education may ultimately be driven by what district officials tell their administrators to offer, while not addressing what educators really need regarding their experiences with students.

A cyclical nature of low self-efficacy among teachers, administrators, and students perpetuates lowered educational experiences. Therefore, a gap in the research was addressed regarding the perceptions educators have with conflict resolution and violence prevention education within their pre-service institutions and current in-service training. The current perceptions of urban high school teachers and administrators uncovered a variety of socially responsive needs. Addressing these needs may lead to future innovative instruction within the pre-service and in-service levels of training for urban high school teachers and administrators.

Summary and Transition

As described in this chapter, the presence or quality of instruction that exists within pre-service and in-service training, and the current perceptions of conflict and violence in school, will assist or impede the impact of preventive education. With numerous health-related antecedents to conflict and violence existing among teenage high school youth (CDC, 2015), students and teachers who receive an education on numerous health-related behaviors may positively identify related characteristics (Tsang, Hui, & Law, 2012). If educators recognize the existence of student health-relat-

SEAN.M. BROOKS, PH.D.

ed behaviors that may lead to victimization, students themselves may be victimized less, thereby increasing their well-being within school (Guimond, Brendgen, Vitaro, Dionne, & Boivin, 2015).

Given the likely existence of pre-service and in-service education for prospective and current teachers and administrators, it is reasonable to state that the quality and focus of that education impacts the existence and perceptions of conflict and violence in school. If formal education was taught to pre-service and in-service educators relating to the health-related antecedents of conflict and violence in school; (a) bullying, (b) cyber bullying, (c) teenage dating violence, (d) teenage substance abuse, (e) teenage depression and suicidal thought; teachers and administrators may prevent, resolve and decrease its existence.

Within Chapter 2, I provide an in-depth understanding on the student health-related antecedents to conflict and violence in school. I examine the theoretical frameworks of self-efficacy (Bandura, 1977), constructivism (Dewey, 1938) and presence of general strain (Agnew, 2006) to describe how the health-related variables impact urban high school students and educators. Finally, within Chapter 2, I describe the interconnection of each health-related variable and the varying perceptions among educators relating to the existence of conflict and violence in school.

Chapter 2

Antecedents to Conflict and Violence in School

According to CDC (2015), sexual behaviors, drug and alcohol use, unintentional injuries, suicide, and physical violence are the leading causes of death among high school students. The prevalence of most health-related behaviors typically occurs across urban high school districts and varies by sex, race, ethnicity, and grade level (CDC, 2015). As school-based violence prevention for students and staff is largely ruled ineffective, programs that focus on social norms and social development may be more impactful (Gavine, Donnelly, & Williams, 2016).

With many studies reflecting the perceptions of students and teachers on current school violence related factors (Bonell et al., 2013; Espelage et al., 2013; Gavine et al., 2016; Perkins, Perkins,

& Craig, 2014), I sought to understand the educational experiences of urban high school teachers and administrators regarding conflict resolution and violence prevention education within their pre-service and in-service teacher training. The perceptions of educators highlighted an absence of applicable conflict resolution and violence prevention education.

This study described an overview of the search strategy conducted during the review the literature. This study highlighted the theoretical and conceptual framework associated with student-based health related issues in school that contribute to the existence of conflict and violence within such environments. Provided is a current exhaustive review of the literature related to (a) bullying, (b) cyber bullying, (c) teenage dating violence, (d) teenage substance abuse, (e) teenage depression and suicidal thought. As these subjects are directly connected to urban high school students (CDC, 2015), this case study sought to understand the experiences educators had at the pre-service levels of teacher training and within in-service professional development.

This review of the literature utilized a comprehensive search strategy that specifically searched for peer-reviewed journals; books, CDC government documents, and health-focused institutional documents (Education Resource Information Center (ERIC), EBSCO Information Services, PsychINFO, Academic Search Complete, the Walden University Online Library and The Centers for Disease Control and Prevention). The peer-reviewed articles included quantitative surveys, qualitative observations and interviews, and longitudinal studies to measure long-term impact. Additionally, the CDC was cited for their domestic statistics and current studies relating to these specified health-related subjects.

The research conducted was focused between the years of 1977 and 2016, with an emphasis on research published on or after 2014. The retained theoretical perspectives dated back to the 1930s and are as current as 2016. This broad timetable allowed for current research to be directly related to the theories utilized for this research.

Three theoretical approaches served as the basis for this research study. The three theoretical approaches included: SET (Bandura, 1977, 1997, 2016), constructivism (Dewey, 1938), and GTS (Agnew, 2001, 2006). These theories are directly related to the presence and influence of health-related factors associated with urban high school students and the education of teachers and administrators within pre-service and in-service training.

SELF-EFFICACY THEORY (SET)

Self-efficacy is defined as the beliefs an individual possesses regarding what they know or do not know (Bandura, 1997). The theory of self-efficacy was developed to examine the factors that contributed to the mastery levels of individuals and their behavioral proficiencies (Bandura, 1997). SET contends that when knowledge is not acquired, self-efficacy decreases, thereby leading to lowered expectations for those we instruct and ourselves (Bandura, 1977). SET also asserts that the sustainability of self-efficacy is based on obstacles presented, expended effort, and adverse experiences; which can all impact personal behavior (Bandura, 1977).

The processes of direct, vicarious, and symbolic sources of information and knowledge require action (Bandura, 1977). Exposure to information can positively impact behavioral patterns within individuals (Bandura, 1977). A lack of meaningful exposure may lead to moral disengagement and feelings associated with a lack of importance on relevant issues (Bandura, 2016).

For teachers and administrators, varying levels of self-efficacy may lead to varying perceptions of student's health-related behaviors within school-based settings (Espelage, Polanin, & Low, 2014; Mercado-Crespo, & Mbah, 2013). Self-efficacy can positively shift when teachers are exposed to impactful violence prevention education that shows understanding and results (Schultes, Stefanek, van de Schoot, Strohmeier, & Spiel, 2014). Bandura (1997) explained that self-efficacy is foundationally constructed through social characteristics, learning situations, and behaviors.

CONSTRUCTIVISM

The foundation of experience and constructing meaning within educational settings describe the theory of constructivism (Dewey, 1938). Constructivist theory explains how one builds on their previous and current experiences to form knowledge. Dewey (1938) explained that experiences could be both educational and counterproductive, depending on the quality of the experience. Furthermore, educators must also drive the learning experiences of their students, and the quality of an educator's experiences may depend on their past and current knowledge (Dewey, 1938).

Based on the theory of constructivism, teachers apply meaning through experience and formal education, thereby leading to an application within school environments. As health-related subjects typically connect to one another, an educator's early exposure or non-exposure to these student-based health issues can impact the rates of conflict and violence within school settings. For example, Powers, Wegmann, Blackman, and Swick (2014) state that educator training, specifically on mental illnesses among students, can help school staff better identify symptoms and intervene. If such education is lacking regarding serious health-related issues, appropriate referrals for care may not be seen nor acted upon (Powers et al., 2014).

General Strain Theory (GST)

General strain theory states that as stressors increase, one is more likely to become aggressive or frustrated (Agnew, 2001). Agnew (2006) states that (a) an inability to achieve desired goals, (b) a threat to, or removal of valued incentives, and (c) anything that presents a threat to an individual; all lead to strain (Agnew, 2006). GST states that these associated factors are more likely to lead one toward crime and many forms of delinquency among both adults and youth, and potentially lead to a dereliction of ones professional responsibilities (Agnew, 2001).

Many factors lead to anger and frustration, such as loss of a family member, verbal taunts, physical assault, a lack of social awareness, or failure to achieve personal goals (Agnew, 2001). For example, bullying can be common among adolescents in school, as can numerous other forms of victimization (Feldman, Ojanen, Gesten, Smith-Schrandt, Brannick, Totura, & Brown, 2014). Victimization and bullying behavior tends to occur more often among those students who fail to adjust to new educational environments or locations (Feldman et al., 2014). Therefore, an increased frustration level that generates anger and dissatisfaction may be present (Feldman et al., 2014). Such feelings can generate behavioral obstacles that also negatively impact academic achievement (Feldman et al., 2014).

Such frustrations and aggressive behaviors may also exist among school staff and lead students to miss school, avoid peer relationships, or engage in violent acts (Dunne, Sabates, Bosumtwi-Sam, & Owusu, 2013). Given the national and global impact of conflict and violence in school-based settings, the health-related predictors of such behavior could be taught within pre-service and in-service training to increase preparedness and prevention.

A complete case study research design should encompass a theory of what is being studied by drawing from what is already known (Yin, 2009). The Youth Risk Behavior Survey or YRBS (CDC, 2015) states that 118 health-related factors impact the well-being of urban high school students. This statement was used as a benchmark for the conceptual framework. While the YRBS (CDC, 2015) solely focuses on urban high school students responding to survey questions regarding health-related subjects, educators themselves are not asked about their experiences with formal education regarding these health-related factors. Therefore, the formal educational experiences of teachers and administrators within pre-service teacher training and in-service professional development was explored regarding these five factors: (a) bullying, (b) cyber bullying, (c) teenage dating violence, (d) teenage substance abuse, (e) teenage depression and suicidal thought. A gap existed in the research regarding the diverse pre-service educational experiences of teachers and administrators for conflict resolution and violence prevention education. This case study investigated the presence and quality of both pre-service training and current in-service professional development for teachers and administrators.

Bullying

I wanted to get this out of the way as quickly as possible. First of all, bullying is a part of life. Every human on earth experiences it. Even if naïve humans believe they have never been bullied, they truly have—they either don't know it or they don't want to admit it. Sadly, evil and a lack of manners and maturity exist in this world and they always have. So, if someone says bullying does not occur in their school, they are either lying, or they are not knowledgeable enough to know better. The simple reason bullying continues to exist in school is because adults are allowing it to happen without proper, harsh, swift consequences. That's it. It's that simple.

The (CDC, 2015) YRBS discovered that many high school youths engage in health-risky behaviors that are associated with the leading causes of death among individuals within the ages of 10-24 years within the United States of America. The (CDC, 2015) YRBS interpretation of the data suggests that high school students in particular engage in a variety of risky behaviors including bullying. However, Blair (2010) emphasized that there are major predictors to bullying, such as the advent of frustration and the onset of aggression. Before the onset of violent behaviors (i.e., bullying), one must first become frustrated and repeatedly stimulated by factors that ignite frustrating feelings (Agnew, 2001). Such feelings and repeated stimuli may ultimately increase the likelihood of aggressive action (Blair, 2010). Moreover, there may be many factors that exist within school classrooms and other school-based environments that stimulate the existence of frustrations that lead to aggressive actions and bullying. Differing perspectives of the existence of frustrating stimuli and aggressive action may contribute to the existence of bullying. Varying perspectives may also impede ones ability to prevent such actions from occurring.

Perceptions of bullying

Bradshaw, Waasdorp, O'Brennan, and Gulemetova (2013) collected data from the National Education Association (NEA) and surveyed 5,064 members comprised of both teachers and school support staff. The results showed that teachers were more likely to witness bullying behaviors than their school support staff counterparts. Teachers were also more likely to have students report bullying incidents to them as opposed to reporting bullying to other school staff members (Bradshaw et al., 2013). Therefore, staff perceptions differ based on levels of exposure to aggressive behavior. Pre-service teachers also report varying perceptions of bullying and their abilities to respond to such episodes (Bauman & Del Rio, 2006; Craig, Bell, & Leschied, 2011). Differing and varied perceptions among pre-service and current educators may also impact the rates of reporting such bullying incidents within school.

As the perceptions of teachers vary regarding the presence of aggression within schools, more students reported acts of bullying combined with a decreased willingness to intervene on such situations (Espelage, Polanin, & Low, 2014). Furthermore, Charmaraman et al., (2013) discovered that teachers are more likely to believe that bullying is a behavior that exists solely among students. In essence, both the perceptions and the reporting of what constitutes violent or aggressive behavior and who is victimized differ in the eyes of students, teachers, and other school staff members.

The perceptions of teachers regarding the treatment of students who identified as lesbian, gay, bisexual, transgender, and questioning (LGBTQ) may also differ (Kolbert, Crothers, Bundick, Wells, Buzgon, Berbary, & Senko (2015). As these teachers reported more knowledge of the policies regarding bullying of LGBTQ students and all students, teachers were more likely to not witness bullying (Kolbert et al., 2015). The less aware teachers were of bullying policies within their school, the more likely they were to witness bullying behaviors, in particular among LGBTQ students

(Kolbert et al., 2015). Given these varying perceptions among educators regarding LGBTQ students, more education is needed to adequately address the witnessing and reporting of bullying episodes (Bradshaw et al., 2013; Charmaraman et al., 2013; Kolbert et al., 2015).

BULLYING WITHIN SCHOOL-BASED ENVIRONMENTS

Examining the locations of where bullying is likely to occur within school-based settings is critical in preventing its existence (Perkins, Perkins, & Craig, 2014). Students report that the highest rates of bullying and harassment occur within hallways, classrooms, and lunchrooms (Perkins et al., 2014). With teachers typically monitoring these locations on an average school day, these specific locations are prevalent within all schools regardless of the school's demographics (Perkins et al., 2014). Furthermore, this may highlight that bullying can occur in any school, regardless of the school's geographic location. School employees must be willing to monitor these locations and assess their own presence within in an effort to prevent further acts (Perkins et al., 2014). While monitoring may especially be true in classroom settings, teachers are responsible for the management of numerous settings where students congregate beyond the classroom.

Classroom instruction could also be detrimental to the levels of learning, specifically relating to the behaviors that are exhibited by both teachers and students (Tobin, Ritchie, Oakley, Mergard, & Hudson, 2013). As the roles of students can become relegated to the point of an observer, teachers may exhibit more control while increasing the frustration levels of the students (Tobin et al., 2013). Furthermore, behaviors and communication techniques between teachers and students should be more fluid and less concrete (Tobin et al., 2013). For example, those who experience strain do so based on the environment in which the strain is occurring (Agnew, 2006). These increased levels of strain that are derived from a specific environmental location may be more likely to drive one toward criminal behavior (Agnew, 2006). This becomes even more likely if a strenuous environment is unavoidable or is forced on an individual with regularity (Agnew, 2006).

RELATIONSHIPS BETWEEN STUDENTS, TEACHERS, AND FAMILIES

Student to teacher relationships are also high predictors of aggressive thoughts and actions among students (Agnew, 2006; Marsh, McGee, & Williams, 2014). These relationships can generate more frustration than those relationships that exist solely between students and their parents (Marsh et al., 2014). Student-to-parent relationships are also significant factors in the aggression levels among students (Marsh et al., 2014). However, the relationships between teachers and students, in particular when dealing with just behavior, are contributors to higher negative feelings (Horan, Chory, Carton, Miller, & Raposo, 2013).

An increase in negativity between teachers and students can lead the student toward antisocial behavior and isolation (Horan et al., 2013). If teachers within school-based settings compounded these aggression levels among their students, aggressive feelings can increase (Marsh et al., 2014). Such feelings are then likely to lead to acts of one bullying others, or being victimized through the act of bullying (Long, 2016). For example, peer victimization is more likely to occur when there are less positive student-to-teacher connections and positive relationships within the classroom (Lucas-Molina, Williamson, Pulido, & Pérez-Albéniz, 2015).

The more aggressive teachers are with their students, the more students report aggression and bullying between their peers (Lucas-Molina et al., 2015). Aggression among teachers and students may alter the willingness of teachers to intervene appropriately in student-to-student victimization or bullying.

Where boys are more likely to report physical aggression, girls are more likely to report feelings associated with aggression and hostility (Tsorbatzoudis, Travlos, & Rodafinos, 2013). If students perceive the behaviors of the teacher as inadequate when addressing bullying situations, student bullying is likely to increase (Lucas-Molina et al., 2015). Such detrimental acts are typically carried out by those deemed as traditional bullies (Lucas-Molina et al., 2015).

Victimization within school-based environments (i.e., classrooms, hallways, bathrooms, locker rooms, cafeterias) can be associated with low levels of family connectedness and school connectedness (Duggins, Kuperminc, Henrich, Smalls-Glover, & Perilla, 2016). While some students can become more vulnerable to victimization through school connections, family connectedness showed to be the more influential factor in decreased levels of aggression and victimization (Duggins et al., 2016). A reassessment of the school culture may also help address the factors that lead to school violence and the antecedents to bullying (Duggins et al., 2016). By letting students contribute to school culture interventions, schools can show growth toward a less aggressive and violent school culture (Bonell et al., 2013).

BULLYING AND HEALTH-RISKY BEHAVIORS

High school students who are deemed bullies are also far more likely to engage in risky health-related behaviors (Long, 2016; Lucas-Molina et al., 2015). These behaviors include taking drugs and alcohol, driving under the influence, cyber bullying, failing class, and vandalizing property (Long, 2016). The more one casually self-reports such personal habits, the more likely they are to engage in bullying and be physically aggressive, in particular if they are of minority status (Mercado-Crespo & Mbah, 2013).

Educating teachers about such behaviors and how to prevent them before they occur, must be apart of the teacher education process at any level (Long, 2016).

CYBER BULLYING

The perpetuation of cyber bullying and victimization has been associated with numerous psychosocial problems such as depression, anxiety, psychological distress, lowered self esteem, lowered self concept, academic problems, and negative school behavior (Dooley, Shaw, & Cross, 2012; Fahy, Stansfeld, Smuk, Smith, Cummins, & Clark, 2016; Fletcher, Fitzgerald-Yau, Jones, Allen, Viner, & Bonell, 2014; Hinduja & Patchin, 2007; Wiederhold, 2014). The CDC's (2015) YRBS reports that 15.5% of students have been bullied electronically (texting, website, e-mail, chat room, instant messaging), over the past 12 months before the survey. The highest rates of cyber bullying occur among white females (26.0%) (YRBS; CDC, 2015), and yet, ironically, many schools force social media participation on their own students as a means of staying connected to peers, their own teachers, and their administrators.

Students who report less satisfaction with their family, dissatisfaction in their socioeconomic status, and less parental monitoring of social media use; are more likely to be cyber bullied (Jun Sung, Jungup, Espelage, Hunter, Patton, Rivers, & Rivers,

2016). Students report that positive school connections and higher school successes are not characteristics that free oneself from face-to-face or online victimization (Jun Sung et al., 2016). Therefore, pressures that students feel to succeed by the school itself can increase the likelihood of student victimization, both face-to-face and online (Jun Sung et al., 2016).

SCHOOL-BASED PERCEPTIONS OF CYBER BULLYING

Perceptions vary regarding the presence of cyber bullying. Students report that technical literacy greatly increases the likelihood of students utilizing technology for cyber bullying purposes (Monks, Mahdavi, & Rix, 2016). While students tend to believe that adult supervision in the home can deter cyber bullying, students have serious doubts about the ability of teachers to monitor such inappropriate use effectively (Monks et al., 2016). Furthermore, cyber-bullying literacy fails to exist within schools largely as a result of teachers not seeing the need for such education, as traditional bullying is commonly viewed as more serious and abundant (Bell & Willis, 2016; Herrera, Kupczynski, & Mundy, 2015).

Bullies engage in cyber bullying in order to hurt another, implore an imbalance of power, or self advertise (Cuadrado-Gordillo & Fernández-Antelo, 2016). Furthermore, victims of cyber bullying perceive its existence due to the need of one person or group of people willfully hurting another (Cuadrado-Gordillo & Fernández-Antelo, 2016; Sari, 2016). Those who are victimized face-to-face are also more likely to engage in social media, thereby increasing the chances of them becoming cyber bullies themselves, or perpetuating their own victimization through online use (Hamer den, Konijn & Keijer, 2014).

Cyber bullying victimization and prevention

Preventing cyber bullying may be both complicated and remarkably simple. As the number of bystanders who witnesses cyber-bullying increase, bystanders are less likely to feel a need to intervene (Obermaier, Fawzi, & Koch, 2016). If there are fewer bystanders who witness cyber bulling, the situation has to be deemed serious enough for one to seek help on behalf of the victim (Obermaier et al., 2016). As a result of impulsivity having a large effect on adolescents within this stage of development (Levesque, 2012), more impulsive bystanders who witness cyber bullying are less likely to help those who are victimized (Erreygers, Pabian, Vandebosch, & Baillien, 2016).

Victims of cyber bullying can also become the bullies themselves (Romera, Cano, García-Fernández, & Ortega-Ruiz, 2016). Increased online usage can also lead to occurrences of online victimization and the reporting of online victimization (Rice, Petering, Rhoades, Winetrobe, Goldbach, Plant, & Kordic, 2015). As a result, it's recommended that online-usage education and curriculum design changes exist for teachers in order to prevent cyber bullying and victimization (Baldry, Farrington, & Sorrentino, 2016). Furthermore, elimination or a limiting of online usage is considered a viable deterrent (Aricak & Ozbay, 2016).

Those who hold negative views of destructive online behavior are far less likely to engage in social media or technological communication (Shim & Shin, 2016). These very individuals are also far less likely to be swayed by their peers, given that pressure to engage in online behavior is ever-present (Shim & Shin, 2016). Moreover, any failure to appropriately self-manage adolescent behaviors online can lead to the formation and perpetuation of cyber bullying (Hamer den & Konijn, 2016).

TEENAGE DATING VIOLENCE

The (CDC, 2015) YRBS states that nationwide, 22.6% of students have engaged in a physical fight one or more times, 7.8% of students have engaged in a physical fight on school property and 2.9% of students who engaged in a physical fight at school needed to be treated by a doctor or nurse; all during the 12-month period before the survey. Nationwide, 5.6% of students had not gone to school one or more days due to fear of being hurt at school or on the way to and from school within 30 days before the survey was taken (CDC, 2015). Of the 68.6% of students who were engaging in dating relationships, 9.6% of them had been physically harmed within those relationships (CDC, 2015; YRBS).

TEENAGE DATING RISK BEHAVIORS

While dating in high school can be common, dating at an early age is correlated with high-risk behaviors and poor academic performance (Orpinas, Horne, Song, Reeves, & Hsieh 2013). Early dating experiences may occur as a result of peer dating pressures before students are developmentally ready (Orpinas et al. 2013). Increased drug use among dating partners and lower positive study habits can also occur as a result of such associations (Orpinas et al. 2013). These dating experiences may result in emotional problems, an unwillingness to detect emotional or physical abuse, drug use, and isolation that can detract from a positive educational experience (Chronister, Marsiglio, Linville, & Lantrip, 2014; Orpinas et al., 2013).

Among students who have dated, 77% report verbal/emotional abuse, while 32% report physical abuse (Niolon, Vivolo-Kantor, Latzman, Valle, Kuoh, Burton, & Tharp, 2015). Girls are also more likely to report such abuses, and the presence of preexisting bullying directly contributed to the existence of violence within these relationships (CDC, 2015; Debnam, Johnson, & Bradshaw, 2014; Niolon et al., 2015; Rothman & Xuan 2014; Vagi, O'Malley, Basile, & Vivolo-Kantor, 2015). If violence exists within a student's family and within the school the student is attending, it's more likely an individual will engage in dating violence (Giordano, Kaufman, Manning, & Longmore, 2015). Given an interest among high school students to date or engage in sexual relationships, students tend to not have adequate extensive experience on how to conduct themselves responsibly within such relationships (Giordano et al., 2015; Lundgren & Amin, 2015).

Teenage dating violence and abuses

Teenage dating violence may begin at the middle school level in the form of sexual harassment (Eom, Restaino, Perkins, Neveln, & Harrington, 2015). Such behavioral exposure may lead to higher rates of physiological impairment at an earlier age, thereby potentially leading to lower rates of mental and emotional health for those students moving on to high school (Eom et al., 2015). Such long-term victimization within dating relationships is also a predictor of substance abuse as one becomes older (Shorey, Fite, Choi, Cohen, Stuart, Temple, & Temple, 2015). Such substance abuse can also become cyclical within dating violence relationships as one becomes older (Shorey et al., 2015).

Mental/emotional, social, and physical victimization is also attributed to alcohol and drug use and the existence of sex within relationships (Lormand, Markham, Peskin, Byrd, Addy, Baumler, & Tortolero, 2013). The presence of these factors can also lead to physical violence within middle and high school dating relationships. With over 50% of middle school students reporting experiences of dating violence, such exposure may led to substance abuse (Lormand et al., 2013; Parker & Bradshaw, 2015; Shorey et al., 2015).

Among high school students, victims of dating violence are more likely to report physiological impairment (i.e., depression and suicidal thought), rather than physical impairment (Coker, Clear, Garcia, Asaolu, Cook-Craig, Brancato, & Fisher, 2014). Such impairment is also attributed to violence within the family, exposure to bullying, and the onset or presence of substance abuse (Coker et al., 2014). Furthermore, victimization through dating violence can dramatically impact the school experiences of students, in particular victimized females and minority students (Chronister, Marsiglio, Linville, & Lantrip, 2014). However, the willingness of students to intervene when dating violence is witnessed in high school is based on efficacy and previous or current educational experiences (Jouriles, Rosenfield, Yule, Sargent, & McDonald, 2016). As high school students receive a formal education on the warning signs and intervention methods to dating violence, their willingness to appropriately intervene and accurately detect warning signs also increases (Jouriles et al., 2016; Williams, Miller, Cutbush, Gibbs, Clinton-Sherrod, & Jones, 2015).

Teenage Substance Abuse

According to the (CDC, 2015) YRBS, over 40 percent of high-school students (grades nine through 12) have used marijuana at least once, and 23.4 percent are considered chronic users of the drug. 22.1 percent of high-school students were offered, sold, or given illegal drugs on school grounds within a 12-month period before the survey (CDC, 2015). Such environments breed an abundance of drug use and sales (Willits, Broidy, & Denman, 2015). Towns and cities that possess middle schools and high schools are more likely to experience the use and sale of drugs; both within school-based environments and within surrounding areas (Willits et al., 2015).

Student drug use within middle school and high school is also commonly associated with bullies and their victims. Bullies are twice as likely to use drugs as opposed to those who are not bullies (Valdebenito, Ttofi, & Eisner, 2015). Victims of bullying are twice as likely to use drugs as opposed to those students who are not bullied (Valdebenito et al., 2015). Such psychological stress is likely to bring about the presence of singular drug use and multiple-categorical dug use (i.e., using more than one drug at one given time) (Di Bona & Erausquin, 2014; Kelly, Chan, Mason, & Williams, 2015).

TEENAGE SUBSTANCE ABUSE RISK FACTORS

Victimization and drug use is also associated with a lack of family support and increased reactive and proactive aggression (Jesús Gázquez et al., 2016). The acceptance level within peer groups also perpetuates drug use (Jesús Gázquez et al., 2016). More specifically, male use of marijuana in high school is directly connected with peer associations, peer discussions related to drug use, deviant behavior, and delinquency (Washburn & Capaldi, 2014). Drug use and associated risk factors may also increase as a student user travels through high school. Growth in both drug use and negative behavior tends to begin among freshman in high school and carry well into their senior year (Washburn & Capaldi, 2014). In relation to bullying and drug use, those who bully are twice as likely to use drugs as compared to nonusers (Ttofi, Farrington, Lösel, Crago, & Theodorakis, 2016).

Seniors in high school are at a higher risk of adult drug use if use persisted throughout high school (Palamar et al., 2014b). For example, marijuana use has show to directly contribute to compromised school relationships, a lack of energy, and lowered school and job performance (Palamar et al., 2014b). Alcohol use among high school students has been directly linked to failing peer relationships, regretful use, regretful behaviors associated with use, and unsafe driving (Li, Simons-Morton, Gee, & Hingson, 2016; Palamar et al., 2014b). Drug use among juniors and seniors in high school also experience higher rates of alcohol and marijuana use one year and beyond after high school (Li et al., 2016). Such use after high school also shows an increase in duel-use (alcohol and marijuana), which is closely associated with increased occurrences of driving while intoxicated or (DWI's) (Li et al., 2016). Higher alcohol use in high school has also been linked to the mixture of alcohol with other liquid substances to increase ease of consumption (Tucker, Troxel, Ewing, D'Amico, & D'Amico, 2016).

Those high school students who are considered poly-drug users (users of more than one drug) and those who consume only alcohol are among the highest risks for dropping out and not completing high school (Creamer, Portillo, Clendennen, & Perry, 2016; Kelly et al., 2015). High school students, who are duel-users of drugs including tobacco, are far more likely than non-users drug users to engage in risky behaviors (Kelly et al., 2015). Single-drug users are also less likely to engage in risky behaviors than their multi-drug using equivalents (Creamer et al., 2016). While alcohol use is the most frequently accepted drug of choice among high school students, not all high school students approve of such drug use (Palamar et al., 2014a).

Teenage substance abuse education

Some school-based programs exist in an attempt to curb drug use among their students. School-based programs have been shown to be more successful among early adolescences as opposed to early childhood (Onrust, Otten, Lammers, & Smit, 2016). Furthermore, addressing the needs of students based on their developmental levels are likely to have a more targeted impact than school-wide programs that attempt a one-size-fits-all approach (Onrust et al., 2016). As all developmental abilities bring different obstacles to peer and group associations, consistent health education at target levels of development show a short-term and long-term positive impact (Bavarian, Duncan, Lewis, Miao, & Washburn, 2015; Onrust et al., 2016). This positive impact is felt among those students who are not already drug users (Bavarian et al., 2015; Onrust et al., 2016). The presence of teenage drug education for teachers and administrators has precise relevance given their frequency of interaction with students within specific stages of development and the presence and rates of drug use within school-based environments.

Teenage Depression and Suicidal Thought

The knowledge pre-service teachers possess regarding mental and emotional disorders among their students is lacking. For example, Kikas and Timoštšuk (2016) state that student teachers may not be exposed to teenage behaviors commonly associated with depression. Novice teachers may only rely on their personal experiences with such conditions to help guide them within student-to-teacher interactions (Kikas & Timoštšuk, 2016). This lack of knowledge may lead a student who is suffering to not come forward with emotional concerns, thereby forcing them into unhealthy isolation (Coles, Ravid, Gibb, George-Denn, Bronstein, & McLeod, 2016; Kikas & Timoštšuk, 2016). Moreover, poor recognition of mental and emotional disorders tends to prevent one from seeking help (Coles et al., 2016). This is also true with regard to teenage dating violence, as high school students who are in volatile relationships are much more prone to depression and suicidal thought (Nahapetyan, Orpinas, Song, & Holland, 2014).

Victimization, teenage depression and suicidal thought

Peer victimization, in particular with bullying, dating violence, and physical violence, also shows an increase in teenage suicide attempts (Crepeau-Hobson & Leech, 2016). Victimization and associated feelings may also not be properly recognized among students. An educator's unawareness of destructive feelings among students has been shown to predict the onset of depression, anxiety, and suicidal thought (Kranzler, Young, Hankin, Abela, Elias, & Selby, 2016). Regarding victimization and aggressive behavior within school environments, victimized students are more likely to suffer from depression, post-traumatic stress disorder (PTSD), and anxiety than those students who victimize (Gumpel, 2016). However, victimizers themselves are more likely to possess traits that are directly linked to PTSD (Gumpel, 2016).

Sexual minority youth are also more likely to experience bullying, thereby leading to an increase in individualized suicidal thought (DeCamp & Bakken, 2016; Mueller, James, Abrutyn, & Levin, 2015). Suicidal thought is mitigated by ones connections to family and peers (Abbott & Zakriski, 2014). However, if victimization leads to suicide, grief among the victims friends may be heightened, thereby leading to pragmatic beliefs that suicide is both practical and not preventable (Abbott & Zakriski, 2014).

EDUCATOR INFLUENCE ON TEENAGE DEPRESSION AND SUICIDAL THOUGHT

Teachers may also exhibit behaviors (i.e., discipline methods, tone of voice, unjust behavior) on students that increase the likelihood of depression and anxiety (Hecker, Hermenau, Salmen, Teicher, & Elbert, 2016). Such practices also lead to suicidal thought and lowered academic achievement among students (Hecker et al., 2016). Harsh and unfair discipline methods toward students can lead to an internalizing of negative emotions, thereby leading to lowered school and personal functioning (Hecker et al., 2016).

Experiencing such behaviors may also lead to an unwillingness or inability to complete school (Melkevik, Hauge, Bendtsen, Reneflot, Mykletun, & Aarø, 2016). Failure to complete school may also compound feelings associated with depression and anxiety well into adulthood (Melkevik et al., 2016). A lack of emotional regulation among students can compound the presence of depression, anxiety and PTSD, thereby generating a cyclical process of mental illness that leads to suicidal thought (Espil, Viana, & Dixon, 2016).

School environments themselves may design the likelihood of increased victimization and mental illness among their students (Evans & Hurrell, 2016). If resources for students struggling with mental illness, such as depression, anxiety, or suicidal thoughts are found lacking, the illnesses may become more hidden among the student population (Evans & Hurrell, 2016; Kranzler et al., 2016). However, teacher-led programs that teach and address mental illness can increase students' knowledge base and assist them in seeking help when symptoms are identified (Lai, Kwok, Wong, Fu, Law, & Yip, 2016). Teacher autonomy and increases in student choice have also shown to lessen the onset of depression and anxiety among students within school-based environments over time (Yu, Li, Wang, & Zhang, 2016). If innovative preventative education is lacking for teachers and administrators who regularly interact with students suffering from such conditions, the recognition of a conditions existence may be absent.

Summary and Conclusions

Bullying, cyber bullying, teenage dating violence, teenage substance abuse, teenage depression and suicidal thought can have far reaching impacts. A lack of education for both teachers and administrators can directly impact the well-being of urban high school students and all students in school-based environments. The presence of health-related issues among teenagers is largely driven by social norms and community acceptance (Bourke, Humphreys, & Lukaitis, 2009). Therefore, the personal perceptions of health-related issues among educators can directly impact the existence of negative or positive health attributes possessed among youth (Bourke et al., 2009). However, pro-social behaviors among teenagers in high school do not ensure an absence in negative health-related habits (Suldo, Gelley, Roth, & Bateman, 2015).

Furthermore, the education for teachers and administrators in both pre-service and in-service educator training is critical. Formal education for teachers and administrators related to the teenage health-related factors mentioned throughout might directly impact the existence or prevention of conflict and violence in school. In addition, current educator perceptions of self-efficacy, constructivism, causes of strain, and knowledge of health-related factors among teenagers can impact the presence of conflict and violence among urban high school students. Any absence in knowledge or formal educational experience of such health-related factors to conflict, violence, or related preventive measures can also impact the future success and safety of students, teachers and administrators.

CHAPTER 3

INVESTIGATIVE APPROACH

The purpose of this study was to understand the perceptions of urban high school educators regarding their educational experiences with conflict resolution and violence prevention education. The previous Chapter highlighted a gap regarding the levels of exposure teachers and administrators have to the health-related factors that are considered antecedents to conflict and violence in school. An exploration of this highlighted gap required a purposeful selection of respondents within a specified location in order to answer the research questions. Therefore, as a case-study researcher, I explored multiple realities (Stake, 1995) while making overviews based on specified evidence (Yin, 2009).

The research design and rational explained the reasoning and design of the study. I described my role as the researcher and explained my individualized participation in the research study, while describing my role and relationships with participants to minimize professional and personal bias. I explained within the methodology section the participant selection, the design and use of instrumentation, and data collection and analysis. Finally, within the last section I addressed the issues of trustworthiness and examined how my research studies design ensured credibility, transferability, dependability and conformability. I also addressed within the final section the procedures to safeguard personal information to confirm that my research study followed suitable ethical procedures.

Case studies should be easily accessible and convenient for the participants, not in an effort to only understand an individual, but rather the existence or absence of a specified element (Stake, 1995). As the researcher I sought to understand the pre-service and in-service educational experiences among 12 urban high school teachers and two administrators regarding conflict resolution and violence prevention education with this single case study. Understanding the past and current educational experiences of teachers and administrators regarding the subjects of conflict resolution and violence prevention in school may help generate innovative instruction within pre-service training and in-service professional development.

This study addressed a gap in the research regarding diverse pre-service training, current episodes of student conflict and violence, and the in-service educational experiences of urban high school teachers and administrators. The pre-service and in-service instruction for educators relating to the antecedents of conflict and violence in school, and a report of their current exposure to such issues among their students may expose a need for innovative training and preventive techniques. Therefore, I explored the following questions:

RQ1 - What are the perceptions of urban high school teachers and administrators during pre-service education relating to conflict resolution and violence prevention?

RQ2 - What are the current experiences of urban high school teachers and administrators regarding student-related conflict and violence in school?

RQ3 - How do urban high school teachers and administrators perceive the effects of in-service conflict resolution and violence prevention education?

My in-depth analysis of the research questions specifically explored the past and current experiences of urban high school teachers and administrators. Furthermore, I sought to understand the perceptions and experiences of urban high school teachers and administrators relating to the antecedents of conflict and violence in school (i.e., (a) bullying, (b) cyber bullying, (c) teenage dating violence, (d) teenage substance abuse, (e) teenage depression and suicidal thought). I obtained this information in an effort to better understand the existence of conflict and violence prevention education within undergraduate preparatory programs and within past and current in-service training.

Through the interview questions, I sought to better understand the pre-service experiences, current experiences, and in-service experiences and perceptions educators have surrounding conflict and violence prevention curriculum and the student health-related factors that contribute. A focus group convened with willing participants at the conclusion of the individual interviews. Clarification regarding interviewee transcriptions and responses were sought during the focus group. The focus group also discussed current examples of conflict and violence among students, while formulating potential strategies and suggestions for future in-service training within the specified case environment.

Within this section, I will describe the qualitative case-study design and approach for this research study. I utilized a purposeful sampling for prospective urban high school teachers and administrators will be used primarily based on their previous pre-service teacher education institution. Secondarily, I selected participants based on the core subject that is currently taught by the teacher (i.e., math, science, history, and literature). I then selected two administrators solely based on their differing pre-service or graduate level teacher education institutions. These two primarily selected groups managed the largest number of students per year within the given case environment.

I individually audio-record interviews, as this was the primary source of data collection, with an audio-recorded focus group accompanying the interviews. Participants also had the opportunity to clarify their interview responses and generate future innovative in-service instructional ideas for their school-based environment. While data analysis was my responsibility, Transcribe.com transcribed the audio-recorded interviews and audio-recorded focus group in writing. These documents were confidential and were not shared with other parties or study participants.

I selected a single-case design given the specified location of an urban high school setting comprised of tenth through twelfth grade students, and the school's proximity to teacher education universities based on the geographic tri-state area. My design was also driven by the research questions, the existence and design of programs, individual decision-making, and the potential need for organizational change (Yin, 2009). Specifically, I explored the perceptions of participants and ask how events exist and what is thought about the presence or lack of those events (Yin, 2009). As the researcher, I also sought to understand the complex experiential interrelationships of participants (Stake, 1995).

While phenomenology was the most similar qualitative approach to the desired research design given the specific existence of an event or series of events, I utilized a case study methodology as I sought to understand a specified case more in-depth (Stake, 1995). Within this study, I sought to understand the perceptions of urban high school educators regarding their pre-service educational experiences with conflict resolution and violence prevention. I also sought to understand the experiences of educators regarding student-related conflict and violence and their perceptions of in-service training. Understanding such perceptions and experiences may help recognize the possible interrelationships between the two educational experiences and how they impact conflict and violence within a specified environment (i.e., urban high school). Based on Stake (1995) and Yin (2009), my proposed research study required a case study methodology. I used face-to-face audio-recorded interviews followed by an audio-recorded focus group to gather data.

During the formal interview process, I gathered the perceptions of educators regarding their previous and current educational experiences while noting their verbal intonation and non-verbal communication. After the professional service company transcribed the interviews and follow-up focus group, I organized the data and coded categories to arrive at generalized themes. I explain the results within Chapter 4.

Although I have been a public school teacher in the past and have taught in a middle school, high school, and university environment, the majority of my time teaching occurred within the middle school grade levels. The formal interviews occurred during the participants planning periods. No incentive came from me directly or indirectly, nor has any arrangement been made with the researcher and the schools administration to compensate participants. While I was aware of personal bias, I field tested the interview questions among experts and professionals who were involved in the education profession at the K-12 public school and university levels of teacher education and had no connection to the research case location or participants.

Methodology

Case study research emphasizes the existence of both education and policy, and how the existence or absence of these can shape an environment (Stake, 1995). Following this model, I structured the current research around the existence of past educational experiences and how these shape behaviors, current educational policies, and instruction for teachers and administrators. Case studies seek to understand the maturation of processes within an industry, the people who work within these environments, and how decisions are structured around a desire to learn (Yin, 2009). Case studies can also demonstrate significant explanations and generalizations across similar environments (Yin, 2009).

The participant pool for this study included 12 urban high school teachers and 2 urban high school administrators whom all worked within the same urban high school building. The participants were currently employed within an urban high school (grades 10-12) within a Midwestern state. The 12 participating teachers represented the core subjects of (a) math, (b) science, (c) history, and (d) literature: as these subjects within this specific case environment see the highest number of students within a single school year. The 2 participating administrators currently held assistant-principal positions and were selected based on their differing graduate level institutional location, as they both graduated from the same undergraduate university.

The selection criterion was purposeful, as I first selected teachers and administrators based on their geographically diverse pre-service undergraduate teacher-education college or university.

Secondly, purposefully selected teachers currently taught a primary core subject (i.e., math, science, history, and literature), one within each grade level (grades 10-12). Specifically within this case environment, the majority of the student population passes through these classes before graduation. Therefore, the teachers who teach core subject content were likely to see more students who represent the studied case environment. However, I primarily selected participants based on their geographically diverse pre-service undergraduate teacher-education college or university. This was done in an effort to diversify the educator's preparatory instructional experiences regarding conflict resolution and violence prevention in school.

Given the number of participants, Stake (1995) suggests having a balance of representation to account for the targeted population. Furthermore, the ultimate purpose of the case approach is to learn (Stake, 1995). As the researcher I achieved this balance while not omitting the participation of teachers or administrators who may have received their pre-service undergraduate teacher-education training from the same college or university. I exhausted the participant list when each grade level and core subject was represented. I selected these participants based on these two sets of criteria alone.

After receiving confirmation from participants and scheduling each interview, I then had participants sign a letter of informed consent to engage in a one-on-one recorded interview and a follow-up focus group. I did not provide the participants the interview questions in advance, nor were the participants compensated for their time.

Instrumentation used in the study included research questions, audio-recorded interviews with the participants, and an audio-recorded follow-up focus group to share transcribed responses, gain clarity for further understanding, discuss current experiences within student-related school violence, and investigate the potential for future innovative in-service training. Eleven preliminary questions were asked. Two of the 11 questions addressed the purposeful participation criteria. Each interview consisted of seven pre-service experiential questions, three educator-to-student interaction questions, and three in-service training questions. I concluded the interview with a time and date where the participant could attend the follow-up focus group while also describing the focus groups primary purpose of clarification, discussing their current experiences within student-related school violence, and investigating the potential for future innovative in-service training.

FIELD-TESTED INTERVIEW QUESTIONS

The research questions, theoretical and conceptual frameworks influenced the interview questions. I field-tested the interview questions due to a lack of previously researched questionnaires that specifically addressed the antecedents of conflict and violence based on pre-service and in-service teacher training. I generated the interview questions and field-tested them among four academic professionals, all of whom worked with pre-service teacher education undergraduate students, high school students, high school teachers, high school administrators, and university professors. The field-tested interview questions guided the one-on-one recorded interviews.

The first 11 questions addressed the preliminary background information about the teachers and administrators. The questions addressed the number of years the participant has taught, the locations in which the participant has taught, the subjects the participant has taught and was currently teaching, their highest degree attained, and where they received their pre-service teacher education training.

The primary interview questions 1-7 focused on research question 1. I designed questions 1-7 to better understand the perceptions and experiences of teachers and administrators regarding their pre-service exposure to conflict resolution and violence prevention education. Questions 1-7 addressed the pre-service experiences urban high school teachers and administrators received regarding teenage health-related antecedents to conflict and violence in school. Interview questions 8-10 addressed research question 2 by examining the current experiences of educators regarding student health-related antecedents to conflict and violence. Interview questions 11-13 addressed research question 3. Interview questions 11-13 explored the perceptions of urban high school teachers and administrator's in-service education regarding conflict resolution and violence prevention in school.

Question 13 specifically asked the participants to rate on a scale of 1 to 10, with 10 being the most important, do they believe a formal education on (a) bullying, (b) cyber bullying, (c) teenage dating violence, (d) teenage substance abuse, (e) teenage depression and suicidal thought—as antecedents to conflict and violence in school, would benefit the staff and students within their school environment. A verbal explanation for the number they choose provided context to more specifically address the question. Appendix A displays the field-tested interview questions for the purposefully selected interview subjects.

Focus Group Analysis

Concluding each designated individual interview, participants were apprised of the follow-up focus group and a suitable date for those willing to participate. A follow-up email was sent to remind all individual willing participants of the agreed upon focus group time and location which took place within a classroom setting. The length of time for the focus group was approximately one hour. Within the focus group I asked for clarification regarding interviewee transcriptions and responses. The focus group participants were asked to discuss their current perceptions of student-related issues regarding conflict and violence in school. Finally, potential strategies and suggestions for future in-service education that were relevant to the case environment were discussed among participants.

Discrepant cases were managed through the process of checking responses based on the existence or absence of specified conflict resolution or violence prevention programs within the participants shared case environment. Accurate recordings of any discrepant cases would resolve any cases where there were drastically differing perceptions during the interview process and focus group. If recognized within the formal interview, follow-up questions would be asked to the designated participants for clarification or a second interview would take place. Discrepant were not foreseen nor occurred within the focus group, as the discussions concentrated on the existence of individual experiences within pre-service training, personal episodes of student related conflict and violence, and a desire for future in-service programs within the specified case environment. Site based in-service training was the same for every school employee within the case environment.

Pseudonyms were used within the results section of this written study in an effort to protect the anonymity of each participant and the name and location of their pre-service institution. However, the state name of the pre-service institution was used to provide geographic context. Minors did not participate in this research study, nor did the urban high school students who inhabited the specified environment. Student names were not used; in particular with relation to interview questions 8, 9 and 10, or any other question where student names arose. This research study did not apply to any other school within the same school district.

My own experience and interest in the antecedents to conflict and violence in school-based settings prompted this research study in an effort to address a gap in the current literature. The interview questions were field-tested to eliminate bias and solely focus on the experiences and perspectives of teachers and administrators within the studied urban high school. I believed this outside input from professional teacher educators regarding the field-testing of questions assisted in the validation process. The removal of bias occurred before the interview process, as the researcher did not solely develop the interview questions.

SUMMARY

I utilized an innovative purposeful selection of teachers and administrators based on (a) the geographically diverse locations of the participant's pre-service undergraduate teacher-education college or university and (b) the grade level and core subject they currently taught (i.e., math, science, history, and literature; grades 10-12). Formal one-on-one interviews solidified the method for data collection. The focus group occurred at a later date to gain clarification from respondents, explore current teacher experiences, and discuss future in-service training options.

Regarding the ethical approaches for this study, maintaining confidentiality in both written and verbal exchanges existed to protect the participants. Additionally, measures involving confidentiality were taken to dissolve any fears related to possible workplace retribution. Discontinuation of answering questions in the formal one-on-one interviews and focus group among respondents were allowed, but did not occur as a related issue. If such an instance had occurred, other prospective participants would have been purposefully selected on the same criteria as before.

CHAPTER 4

EDUCATOR EXPERIENCES, INVESTIGATIVE DISCOVERIES AND RESULTS

When conducting interviews in a case study, participant's diverse experience can lead to a robust interpretation of results (Stake, 1995). While educators come from diverse preparatory programs, they also experience numerous social situations with their current students, and they receive varying degrees of in-service education within those locations. Researchers have indicated that educators have varying perceptions regarding student health-related factors (i.e., psychological) that contribute to conflict and violence in school (Bradshaw et al., 2013; Bushman et al., 2016). However, research has not examined educator's perceptions of their pre-service and in-service levels of training and whether or not their current experiences with students align with such training methods. Therefore, the existing gap in research raises the question: What are urban high school educator's perceptions of their pre-service and in-service conflict resolution and violence prevention education?

This research study centered on three research questions to address this gap:

Research Question 1: What are the perceptions of urban high school teachers and administrators pre-service education relating to conflict resolution and violence prevention?

Research Question 2: What are the current experiences of urban high school teachers and administrators regarding student-related conflict and violence in school?

Research Question 3: How do urban high school teachers and administrators perceive the effects of in-service conflict resolution and violence prevention education?

This chapter includes the research setting for participant selection, the demographics of the participants, and the data collection. Furthermore, this chapter includes the analysis of the data that was collected and issues with trustworthiness. Additionally, the connections between the studies theoretical and conceptual framework, and the selected participant responses to individual interview questions and a follow-up focus group are discussed throughout. A discussion of the results and a summary will conclude Chapter 4.

RESEARCH SETTING

This case study included a single urban high school within a Midwestern state. This urban high school had roughly 2,000 students enrolled, grades 10-12. There was a neighboring freshman building that housed ninth grade students only, however, ninth grade educators were not included within this study. All participants for this study worked in the main high school building, grades 10-12. In the research year of 2017, this studied urban high school employed 187 staff members, 115 of which held the title of classroom teacher. There were five assistant principals (administrators) and one head principal. The student body was almost evenly divided (51% male, 49% female) and 71.9% of the student population is Caucasian. This Midwestern urban high school had a graduate rate of 78% in the 2016-2017 school year. This Midwestern urban high school is the only high school in the school district.

The location of the 12 individual teacher interviews took place within the participating teachers' individual classrooms. The two assistant administrator interviews were conducted within their individual offices. There were no other participants or individuals present during the individual interviews and the door was closed in each room and office to ensure privacy.

The follow-up focus group was made up of eight teacher participants from the previous individual interviews. The focus group convened inside a conference room within the case environment. All 14 interview participants were apprised of the focus group date and time. However, four teachers were not present. One of the four teachers contacted me in advance to let me know they would be absent. Both assistant administrators were not present for the follow-up focus group. The focus group occurred within a classroom inside the case-studied location.

DEMOGRAPHICS

The study environment included a student body that was almost evenly divided (51% male, 49% female). 73.8% of the student population was Caucasian, while 12.9 % was African American, 9.2% was Hispanic, and 0.7% was Asian. This Midwestern urban high school had a graduate rate of 78% in the 2016-2017 school year. The case-studied Midwestern urban high school is the only high school in the school district. There are eight elementary schools, two middle schools, one freshman building, and one technical center within the school district.

A letter was emailed to the schools head principal to elicit cooperation in this research study. I individually emailed all core teachers within each grade to elicit their participation. Two criteria for participation included: (a) the geographically diverse location of the participant's pre-service undergraduate teacher-education college or university; and (b) the subject and grade level the participating educator taught. I attained one core teacher per subject and grade (i.e., math, science, history, and literature; grades 10-12) for participation. In total 12 teachers were interviewed along with two assistant administrators.

The 12 participating teachers came from nine different pre-service teacher-education undergraduate institutions, spanning across five different states within the United States. Three of the participating teachers graduated from the same pre-service undergraduate teacher-education institution, while two other participating teachers graduated from the same pre-service undergraduate teacher-education institution that differed from the previous three teachers. Both assistant administrators graduated from the same pre-service undergraduate teacher-education institution, however, they differed on the location and institution of their graduate level degree that qualified them to attain the role of assistant administrator.

Pseudonyms were used for each of the participants, the location of their pre-service undergraduate degree and graduate school degree when applicable, and all information remained confidential. Table 1 contains demographic information of each teacher and assistant administrative participant. Table 2 contains the participant's undergraduate degree earned and the state location of their pre-service undergraduate college or university. Table 2 also shows the assistant administrators graduate school state location. Both participating assistant administrators earned their undergraduate degrees from the same institution. However, their graduate degrees that qualified them to be assistant administrators were attained from differing institutions within differing states.

TABLE 1

Participant Demographics (pseudonyms), Grade Taught, Highest Degree Earned, and Years of Teaching Experience.

Name	Gender	Teaching Position	Highest degree	Years Taught
Damon	M	10th grade Math	Masters	11
Mary	F	10th Grade Science	Masters	7
Margret	F	10th Grade History	Bachelors	2
Erin	F	10th Grade Literature	Bachelors	7
Sally	F	11th Grade Math	Masters	7
Alice	F	11th Grade Science	Masters	14
Matt	M	11th Grade History	Masters	10
Betty	F	11th Grade Literature	Bachelors	6
Jasmine	F	12th Grade Math	Bachelors	1
Kristen	F	12th Grade Science	Bachelors	19
Macy	F	12th Grade History	Bachelors	12
Shannon	F	12th Grade Literature	Masters	30
Mitch	M	Administrator	Masters	13
Janice	F	Administrator	Masters	14

TABLE 2

Participant Demographics (pseudonyms), Participant Degree Earned, Pre-service Undergraduate University (UNV), Administrative Graduate University (AGUNV), and State.

Name	Gender	Degree Earned	UNV or AGUNV Institution/State
Damon	M	Accounting	University (UNV) 1 (OH)
Mary	F	Biology	University (UNV) 2 (OH)
Margret	F	Psychology	University (UNV) 3 (IA)
Erin	F	English Ed.	University (UNV) 4 (OH)
Sally	F	Math Ed.	University (UNV) 5 (TN)
Alice	F	Science Ed.	University (UNV) 1 (OH)
Matt	M	History Ed.	University (UNV) 6 (OH)
Betty	F	English Ed.	University (UNV) 1 (OH)
Jasmine	F	Math Ed.	University (UNV) 7 (MI)
Kristen	F	Science Ed.	University (UNV) 4 (OH)
Macy	F	History Ed.	University (UNV) 8 (IN)
Shannon	F	Literature Ed.	University (UNV) 9 (TN)
Mitch	M	Social Studies Ed.	University (UNV) 1 (OH) / Administrative Graduate University (AGUNV) 1 (OH)
Janice	F	Physical /Health Ed.	University (UNV) 1 (OH) / Administrative Graduate University (AGUNV) 2 (AL)

DATA COLLECTION

Participant Selection

Participant's background information was gathered to solidify the two prerequisites for the purposeful sampling criteria. Participants responded back to me via email and phone call to confirm their possible participation. Once the preliminary prerequisites were verified and all willing participants had responded, confirmation of their participation in the study was agreed upon.

Of the 36 teachers that were initially contacted, 12 teachers agreed to participate. This solidified the second selection criteria of grade level taught and subject matter. While some participants graduated from the same pre-service undergraduate institution, nine participants graduated from differing pre-service teacher-education undergraduate institutions. Two assistant administrators agreed to participate among the available four, as the fifth assistant administrator was out town. Once this preliminary information was gathered, the audio-recorded one-on-one interviews were scheduled with each volunteer participant.

Interviews

I interviewed 12 teachers in their individual classrooms and two assistant administrators in their individual offices. While we agreed that each audio-recorded interview would last roughly one hour, each teacher interview lasted roughly 30 minutes. The two interviews involving the administrators were the shortest, lasting roughly 17 to 20 minutes long. I audio-recorded each interview on two separate digital audio-recording devices. After each interview, I saved, copied, and converted each file into an MP3 audio file for storage under a password encrypted audio-storage device. A transcription service converted each Mp3 audio file/interview into a multipage Microsoft Word ™ document. The transcription service concluded their transfer from digital audio to text within two days. I also took notes while listening to the audio-recordings and while reading the transcriptions for accuracy and clarification. I began the coding process during this time. Common codes emerged when while listening to the audio-recorded interviews and reading the corresponding transcriptions. Similarities were highlighted and a list of codes was developed. Themes emerged from each list of codes based on each set of interview responses that corresponded to the appropriate research question. I did not encounter any variation in the strategies and methods defined within Chapter 3. There were no unusual incidents that occurred during the interviews. No participant withdrew their participation at the beginning, during, or at the conclusion of the individual audio-recorded interviews.

Focus Group
A focus group convened seven days after participants concluded the interview portion of the study. All participants were apprised of the focus group meeting in advance at the conclusion of their individual interviews, along with a follow up email. Eight teachers attended the focus group with three teachers not attending, and one teacher letting me know in advance they would not be in attendance. The assistant administrators were not in attendance. Neither assistant administrator provided an explanation or correspondence that described the reasoning for their absence. The focus group reexamined research questions 2 and 3, as these are specific to the case study. Not every teacher within the focus group participated, but the teachers spoke one at a time and provided insight as to what concerns they have regarding the student-health related antecedents to conflict and violence in school (research

question 2) and their thoughts on the current state of their in-service training (research question 3). Responses were then triangulated with the teacher's previous responses from the individual interviews. The teacher's responses within the focus group were also triangulated with the assistant administrators previous responses from the individual interviews.

Data Analysis

Useful and purposeful operations can help place data in a preliminary order (Yin, 2009). Therefore, a case study researcher can never substitute for having a general strategy in place from the beginning (Yin, 2009). In this research case, the potential for an organizational-level logic model presented itself as a series of events over a standard period of time showed particular patters of discovery (Yin, 2009). Focusing on this approach from the beginning allowed me to examine the theoretical and conceptual framework from the formation of the research questions to the generation of individual interview questions. As stated in Chapter 3, the use of Microsoft Word™ or Microsoft Excel™ would primarily be used for this analysis regarding pattern matching and explanation building (Yin, 2009) until common themes quickly emerged.

As stated in Chapter 3, specified vocabulary was introduced to participants through the interview questions based on the conceptual framework (i.e., bullying, cyber bullying, teenage substance abuse, teenage dating violence, teenage depression and suicidal thought). This framework was interwoven within the individual interview questions and provided a common analysis based on each participant. While the same vocabulary was used with each participant, pre-coding did not take place as to avoid bias within the study as themes were generated after the analysis of the interviewers responses.

The analysis of the interviews started with listening to the audio-recorded interviews and then sending them to the transcriber. Once I received the transcriptions, the audio-recorded interviews were listened to again to verify the accuracy of the transcriptions and interview responses. There were no discrepancies between the audio-recorded interview responses and the transcriptions.

I organized the interview responses based on the individual interview questions, which were previously aligned with the research questions. First, respondent's answers were highlighted from one participant to the next. Common codes were generated across each individual interview question response that corresponded to each research question. These codes were themed based on each individual research question. Cross coding occurred between teachers' interview responses and assistant administrators responses. Numerous themes emerged for each research question. These themes were then shared with participants who attended the focus group. Themes were verified for their accuracy among focus group participants, and there were no discrepancies reported by participants based on the generated themes for each research question.

Focus group responses were aligned with Research Questions 2 and 3. Only eight teachers attended the focus group. Their responses were audio-recorded and transcribed. After receiving the transcriptions, I verified the audio-recorded responses while reading the transcriptions. Focus group data was triangulated with the individual interview responses of both participating teachers and assistant administrators.

An organizational-level logic model was developed at the conclusion of the focus group. This model chained events regarding the responses of research questions 2 and 3 as compared to the existing case environment's vision statements and the offered in-service training for educators. Inputs, and outputs within this case environment were highlighted, while looking for consistencies and inconsistencies (Yin, 2009). Logic models also seek to clearly align the vision of the organization based on their perceived goals, current inputs, outputs, and future desired goals (Yin, 2009). An analysis was drawn to emphasize any discrepancies regarding the case environments vision statements and the currently offered in-service training. This was then compared to the current experiences of teachers and their desired future in-service training. These findings could then be delivered back to the studied case for stakeholder consideration.

Evidence of Trustworthiness

Case study credibility involves designing questions that begin with the origin of a participant, while ultimately leading to specific procedures employed within the given environment (Yin, 2009). Locations of the participating teachers and administrator's pre-service undergraduate institutions were disclosed during the recruitment phase and discussed throughout the interview process. Audio-recorded interview responses and the audio-recorded focus group responses established the credibility of participant's responses and connection to the research questions. Triangulation was established in an effort to corroborate participants responses (Yin, 2009), based on educators experiences student health-related antecedents to conflict and violence and the offered in-service training within the case environment.

The in-service education was the same for each participant, as each school staff member received and attended the same required training. All individual participants confirmed the existence of both Restorative Practices and *ALICE* Training (Alert, Lockdown, Inform, Counter, and Evacuate) (*ALICE* Training Institute, 2017) in-service education for teachers and administrators within the district and the studied case environment. The organizational-level logic model provides an analysis of case study administrative inputs and the desired teacher outputs for future in-service training.

Most case studies do not allow for transferability. However, depending on the generalizations or purposeful sampling used; some transferability may be applicable (Stake, 1995). Pre-service experiences could be shared with other pre-service undergraduate teacher education institutions to help design future educational experiences. The same could be said for current school-based in-service programs and educator's desired forms of professional development.

As previously described, all data remained in my possession on encrypted and password protected audio-recording devices throughout the entire interview, focus group, and analytical process. All audio-recorded data was only shared with the professional transcription company and then returned to me within three days. Notes were taken by me throughout the individual audio-recorded interview process and audio-recorded focus group to highlight generalizations and common themes. Although, notes were not taken the entire time as to not distract from the questions and answers being recorded.

Pre-structured formats before data gathering can increase objectivity and remove bias (Yin, 2009). Therefore, the preliminary selection basis for participants within this study made a successful attempt in diversifying the pre-service backgrounds of teachers and administrators. The individual interview questions were field tested among four teacher education professionals with diverse experiences and educational backgrounds. The interview process was free of personal biases and any previous experiences I have personally had. The results section discusses the research questions that aligned with the discovered themes and the participants' responses. These generated themes were then shared with those who attended the follow-up focus group to measure validity. There were no discrepancies between participant interview responses and the generated themes that were aligned with the research questions.

Study Results

This section examines the results of the current research study, specifically organized by the research questions. Each interview question was organized and aligned appropriately with each research question. As themes emerged through coding and cross coding the participant responses, themes emerged that aligned with the research questions.

Research Question 1

Individual interview Questions 1-7 (Appendix A) aligned with and supported research question 1. These interview questions directly addressed participants pre-service perceptions, specifically related to the presence or absence of conflict resolution and violence prevention education and the student health-related antecedents to violent behavior (i.e., bullying, cyber bullying, teenage substance abuse, teenage dating violence, teenage depression and suicidal thought). Four emerging themes were generated through the coding process (Figure 1).

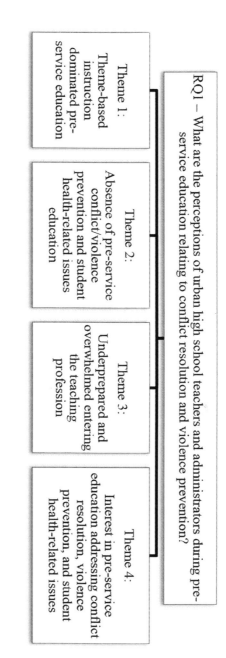

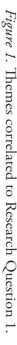

Figure 1. Themes correlated to Research Question 1.

Theme 1: Theme-based instruction dominated pre-service education. Interview question 1 specifically addressed the previous experiences and perceptions teachers and administrators had regarding their pre-service instruction. While 13 participants recalled heavy instruction on their subject content, Mary and Damon were the only participants who failed to receive any formal educational instruction whatsoever in the actual field of educational theory during her undergraduate work. Following her Bachelors Degree attainment in Biology, Mary received her teaching certification through her graduate level work, which lasted one-year, followed by a student teaching experience and the attainment of a Masters Degree. Damon received his Bachelors Degree in Accounting and didn't receive any educational instruction until his graduate schoolwork, where he ultimately attained a Masters Degree in Educational Leadership from the same institution as his undergraduate degree. For the remaining 12 participants, their pre-service course work involved learning their specified subject matter and receiving formal instruction on how to teach their subject matter. Erin's response summarized many of the other 12 participants experiences when she stated,

It was basically just the fundamentals of how to be a teacher, and setting up your lesson plans, and setting up your objectives, and following the state standards. That was kind of the core background of it. It was kind of a "learn as you go" situation.

Jasmine described her pre-service instruction in a similar manner:

It was mainly focused on teaching the content. I took two year's worth of math methods courses. So that was the bulk

of my education. I did do, like, an Ed Psychology, a class on diversity, a class focused on reading and literacy, and then one class on kind of classroom management type stuff. Mainly, the focus was on, "How do you teach your content area?"

The two participating assistant administrators described their pre-service course work in the field of education. Mitch stated, "It was in theory and some practice. Obviously, with the structural piece of lesson planning and, obviously, the student teaching piece. I really feel I was very, very limited with special education, very limited." Janice's response was similar when she stated, "Just a lot of content. Not necessarily specific stuff. I don't remember a whole lot of stuff. Again, my point with that, as well as with my other degrees, you don't learn until you're in it."

Janice firmly believed, throughout the entire interview process, that she couldn't learn unless she was actually participating in the act. She also believed the same for many teachers within the case environment. Initially, she seemed to disregard the importance of formal education for herself, yet she believed it could be beneficial for others.

Theme 2: Absence of pre-service conflict/violence prevention and student health-related issues education. Interview questions 2-6 specifically addressed the presence of pre-service course work or workshops specifically dedicated to the topics of conflict resolution, violence prevention, and the student health-related antecedents to conflict and violence in school (i.e., bullying, cyber bullying, teenage substance abuse, teenage dating violence, teenage depression and suicidal thought). Each participant described their experiences in their own distinctive way. However, all participants described an overwhelming lack of formal educational instruction and workshop opportunities on all of the student health-related antecedents to conflict and violence in school. For example, Damon, Matt, and Jasmine described their experiences when asked about the presence of pre-service coursework (or graduate coursework in the case of Damon) related to conflict resolution and violence prevention. Damon stated,

> *No. Not even close. I think they're doing a significant disservice to teachers by not preparing them for the realities of what they're going to experience when they get into the classroom. There was nothing that we were asked to do, other than—we did some observations, obviously—went out and observed—but nothing dedicated to school violence.*

Matt agreed by stating,

> *No. There was not. Most of the focus was on instruction methods, and anything to do with that was maybe brought up in a side discussion, or maybe in passing, but nothing — at least that I can remember — was focused on that specifically.*

Jasmine also agreed, but stated that classroom management was the only course that ever came close to covering anything related to conflict and violence in school:

> *No. In my classroom management class, for lack of a better word, during my internship because we were all in urban schools, sometimes that came up. So, we kind of were thrown into the fire, and then talked about how we dealt with the situation and what we could do moving forward. When there were instances where stuff like that happened, we talked about*

it but it wasn't an intentional – like, "we need to discuss violence and dealing with conflict."

Regarding the presence of workshops on issues involving conflict and violence in school, the presence of organized curriculum and specified coursework was absent for participants within their pre-service education. However, while some workshops did exist on specified issues on their campuses, none of the workshops were related to conflict and violence in school, nor were they attended by any of the participants. Betty described one experience, which matched that of many, when she described passively learning a few things regarding violence among African American males:

I can't remember anybody that specifically came in to talk about that. I know we did read a book in one of my classes that was talking about 'Teaching Literature To Black Adolescent Males,' and that book specifically talks about violence among the black community and the male community, but no one came in with that.

When participants were asked about bullying, cyber bullying, teenage substance abuse, teenage dating violence, teenage depression and suicidal thought being covered within their pre-service education, their descriptive answers varied. While some participants briefly discussed exposure to a specific topic, they were only brought up by one of their fellow classmates or peers, or in a casual nature typically introduced to them in passing. Participants responded by stating that no formal class existed that specifically discussed these issues, nor did any pre-service professor spend any length of time covering how to spot such episodes that may lead to violent behavior and how to manage them if they arose. Margret's lack of experience was common, and one that was shared by others when she stated,

> *I think the only one we might have touched on a little bit was cyber bullying, actually, in a technology course where we learned how to use technology in the classroom and like monitoring proper student use. Otherwise again, all of those I would say we touched on very briefly in one management course, probably only for a day and that was it.*

Betty described her experience by stating that some of these topics were covered, but only briefly, when she stated,

> *I guess specifically we talked about bullying in there, and how in an inclusion setting, or mainstream, how people will tend to bully special education students more. I know there were times when we did talk about depression and dating violence and suicidal thoughts within group discussions, just among us students, Not as much substance abuse, though.*

Betty's response was also common among participants in that if these topics were discussed, they took place among the pre-service undergraduate students themselves describing their own experiences or classroom observations. However, there was an overall absence of formal education on these student health-related antecedents to conflict and violence, in particular when coming from college or university professors.

The administrative responses were also similar regarding any previous education related to student health-related antecedents to conflict and violence, Mitch responded by stating,

The only thing I would say maybe would be bullying. Student relationships bleed through a lot of that anyway. Nothing specific like, "Okay, today we're going to talk about bullying and how to address it in the classroom. How do you address it without crossing the line with students? When do you address it with your administrator?" Nothing in terms of specifics with it.

Janice's pre-service background was in physical education. Regarding her background with being formally taught these student health-related antecedents to conflict and violence, she stated,

A lot of my content was in P.E. (Physical Education). I'm sure some of those themes were interwoven, but again, cyber-bullying, I can definitely tell you no. Maybe it scratched it, but not to the extent of the level where it is now.

The assistant administrators had the largest amount of experience with these student health-related antecedents to conflict and violence, but they revealed that they were only slightly introduced to these subjects within their graduate level coursework that qualified them to be administrators. When asked about his graduate work and whether it covered these student health-related topics (i.e., bullying, cyber bullying, teenage substance abuse, teenage dating violence, teenage depression and suicidal thought) Mitch stated,

Yes. I would say probably one of the strongest courses that I had was my school law course. Dug deep into really looking at how cyber-bullying relies on just social media. In terms of actually dealing with it within the classroom, not as much, no.

Janice also stated that she had more experience with these subjects in graduate school coursework. However, not all subjects were covered. She stated,

> *Depression, yes. Dating violence, yes. Suicidal thoughts, yes. I don't necessarily know about substance abuse. Maybe scratch surface on cyber-bullying, but bullying, yes. Those were pretty interwoven in my school counseling degree. A little bit when you're talking about educational leadership, the laws behind those things. Yes, but again, I'd point back to you don't know what you know until you're in it.*

Janice's perspective consistently indicated that formal education could only take you so far. Her belief was that if a formal education on these topics is not present, it simply takes experience to make one more familiar and educated. In particular when she stated on more than two occasions, "you don't know what you know until you're in it."

Theme 3: Underprepared and overwhelmed entering the teaching profession. Participants were then asked about their student teaching experiences and whether or not they were exposed to these student health-related issues as a student teacher. Their examples of student-related conflict and violence in school were remarkably serious. For example, Damon described his student teaching experience by stating,

> *I had a student commit suicide in my third week of student teaching. I had no idea what to do. I mean, I had no idea! I didn't now how to talk to the kids. I didn't know how to talk to myself. I didn't know what to think.*

I remember struggling, really struggling. The minute I stepped foot in the classroom, the first day, those things smacked me right in the face.

Sally described her student teaching experience regarding these student health-related issues by stating,

I went into the alternative school and I saw everything that you would expect to see there. It was really rough first placement for me because I left thinking every day like this is what I want to be doing? I'd say that the only real aspect of that would have been like fighting and aggression is what I witnessed there and I wasn't prepared. I wasn't comfortable with that at all.

Matt described his unpreparedness in student teaching, specifically regarding these student health-related issues, by stating,

Student teaching-wise, if I had encountered that, I would have been probably unprepared, for the lack of training on that. We didn't have any education on most of those topics, so it was kind of — you know, very 'feet to the fire' and 'learn as you go' at that time.

Jasmine and Sharon also had difficult experiences in their student teaching regarding their lack of preparedness. Jasmine described her student teaching experience by stating,

Well I mean there was a fight in my classroom. It was between one of my students and then a girl who was not one of my students. She just came into the classroom and started attacking

my student. I had no idea what to do. My mentor teacher wasn't in the room because he was dealing with a student I'd already kicked out for behavioral problems. I taught very underprepared, and I was like, "I have no idea what to do."

When asked about her student teaching experience and being taught about conflict resolution and violence prevention in school, Sharon stated,

Underprepared. I personally struggled just with any kind of confrontation, so that to me wasn't an easy situation. There were a couple of times, yes, that I encountered bullying. I, unfortunately, had a cooperating teacher. He was at the end of his career. He was very burned out, I could tell. As far as going beyond that, no, unfortunately. Unfortunately, because I really would have liked to.

Neither administrator could recall their student teaching experiences, nor could they point to any particular instance where they had to manage bullying, cyber bullying, teenage substance abuse, teenage dating violence, teenage depression and suicidal thought during that time. However, they both did state that these were not subjects brought to their attention by their cooperating teacher, thereby showing a similarity to the teachers responses given a lack of preparedness and continued education on these subjects.

Theme 4: Interest in pre-service education addressing conflict resolution, violence prevention, and student health-related issues. Every teacher and administrative participant except Alice stated that there should be a serious in-depth formal education on the topics of conflict resolution, violence prevention, and the student health-related antecedents to such behaviors within pre-service teacher preparation courses and curriculum. Regarding Alice's uncertainty of what course work that addressed these issues would look like, Alice stated: "I don't even know how well that could really be taught in a classroom. It's more of a situational thing. I'm not sure how you would be able to do that. That's hard."

When asked about possible recommendations for pre-service education regarding conflict resolution and violence prevention in school, Damon stated,

> *I think we have to. As an education community, we have to start dedicating more time to it. It's reality. I think one could write a course on it. I think one could teach a course on it.*

Margret agreed, by stating,

> *Definitely. We didn't have anything that prepped us for the kind of issues you have to deal with day-to-day with students and what they struggle and go through. I didn't get any kind of prep for that in my training as a teacher at my college. I think there's just a void right now in education that teachers are not given those tools to deal with mental health issues in the classroom.*

Kristen also agreed and was even more direct when she stated,

> *There probably should be an entire course dedicated to just violence in school. If there's cyber bullying and it's happening after hours, is that something that the school is allowed to touch? I think it would be beneficial for a teacher to know where the lines are drawn and what kind of action we can take at the school for things that happened off school grounds. I think*

that should be covered even before ever going in for methods, because if you're in a school and you have no clue about any of that, that's putting somebody in a serious situation.

As a 30-year veteran of the teaching procession, Sharon agreed that such an education on these issues is critical within the pre-service level of teacher training. Sharon stated,

I definitely believe there should be a course on it, and not just lecture, but to be involved in simulating the situations, because we can all say this is how I'd react until you're actually in that situation, especially if you're talking about someone that could resort to bullying or violence.

Both assistant administrators answered in a more in-depth manner, given that they both admitted dealing with and managing student discipline on a daily basis, specifically regarding bullying, cyber bullying, teenage substance abuse, teenage dating violence, teenage depression and suicidal thought. Mitch stated:

I think, especially coming from a safety aspect, the majority of the country is moving towards ALICE training. I think, looking at school violence, that aspect absolutely. In terms of bullying, I feel that you need to understand what bullying is and the proper statutes that go along with it, because if you look at the way it is today, every parent wants to throw bullying up. First-day incident, 'My kid's being bullied.' Cyber-bullying, my god! We see it so much as an administrator, daily. We have kids that will go into physical conflict without ever having said one word to one another face-to-face.

As Mitch referenced *ALICE* Training, this form of training is common within most school districts, even if it's known by another name in another geographic location. *ALICE* Training within this case environment is primarily a procedural process for "locking down" a building in the instance of a possible school shooter or another illegal disruption, inside or outside of a school building or campus. *ALICE* Training is not a preventative measure for the student health-related antecedents to conflict and violence in school, such as bullying, cyber bullying, teenage substance abuse, teenage dating violence, teenage depression and suicidal thought. *ALICE* Training is solely a procedural event.

Janice also adamantly agreed with Mitch and other teachers regarding the importance of pre-service training and formal education on these issues:

> *Educating and bringing in the components about social media and cyber-bullying, I think that's huge. I think that should be a class that teachers take, especially when you're talking about secondary education. I think that needs to be something that's pointed out to teachers about how to deal with it, because it's real and it's here and it's now. I think sometimes undergrad courses are very content-driven. You don't necessarily teach those people skills. It's very important.*

The assistant administrators strongly believed that a formal education on the topics of conflict, violence, and the student health-related antecedents to conflict and violence in school should be taught within the pre-service level of teacher training. Assistant administrators also believed that the teachers they were currently responsible for observing and evaluating needed this training, as it might make both administrative jobs easier and those teachers they're responsible for more successful.

Research Question 2

Individual interview questions 8-10 (Appendix A) aligned with and supported research question 2. These interview questions directly addressed teachers and administrators current or past experiences specifically relating to student interactions involving the student health-related antecedents of conflict and violence (i.e., bullying, cyber bullying, teenage substance abuse, teenage dating violence, teenage depression and suicidal thought). The participant's perceptions of where they received their current skills to manage or recognize such factors, and their perceptions of their fellow co-workers abilities to recognize and manage similar situations, were also sought. Three emerging themes were generated through the coding process (Figure 2).

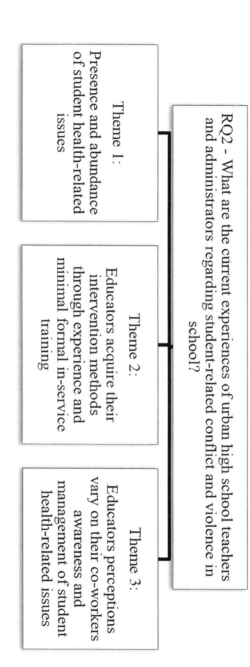

Figure 2. Themes correlated to Research Question 2.

Theme 1: Presence and abundance of student health-related issues. Interview question 8 specifically addressed the previous experiences teachers and administrators had regarding interactions with student health-related antecedents of conflict and violence while employed (i.e., bullying, cyber bullying, teenage substance abuse, teenage dating violence, teenage depression and suicidal thought). Regarding all of these behaviors, both assistant administrators were the only participants who disclosed that they observed and managed every behavior listed, on a daily basis. Teacher's responses varied, as not every teacher has dealt with or witnessed every behavior. However, the student health-related antecedents to conflict and violence in school that were mentioned by teachers and administrators were done so in detail. Specifically regarding bullying, Margret summarized many teachers responses by stating,

Bullying is something you have to deal with day-to-day as a teacher. Kids making snide comments to each other and not behaving in a way that's appropriate or respectful. So bullying is a daily thing.

Macy believed that cyber bullying dominated any form of bullying within school. She stated, "I think most bullying at the high school is done over Facebook, Twitter, and Instagram." Damon agreed with the cyber bullying problem by stating, "I mean, with Twitter and Facebook and Snapchat — don't even get me started on Snapchat — in instances of cyber bullying, and the…ugh. Nauseating."

While bullying is a serious issue and one that teachers and assistant administrators recognized as being a problem, cyber bullying appeared to take precedence as a potential precursor to an actual violent physical act.

Alice, Damon, Jasmine, and Macy all reported witnessing and dealing with student-related dating violence. Alice described how she manages dating violence by stating: "I've had students that I've seen where their boyfriends, in the hallway, will grab them by the throat. Again, I just report … just report, report, report."

Damon described an incident that occurred in the hallway, when he said:

I had an encounter the other day. I'm walking back and I see a young man grab a young lady by the arm, and I was like, "We don't do that." He was irate with me. The behavior that he exhibited in that instance is the same behavior that he's going to exhibit outside of here. I don't know how to fix that. I can stop him, right? "Don't touch her like that. We don't do that here," you know? I can have a conversation with the young man, like, "That's not how men behave. We don't put our hands on women in anger, ever." I've got 25 seconds to talk to this kid. He's had 15 years of watching it happen at home.

Jasmine described an incident of dating violence with a student of hers and how the student's councilor wasn't available for consultation. Jasmine stated:

There was some emotional abuse going on. She just came to my class sobbing. I was like, "Here, you go out in the hallway. Let me get class started," and I went out and talked with her. I had asked her, "Have you checked with your counselor?" She had, but her counselor wasn't available. I felt like I just couldn't leave her there.

Macy also described an incident that occurred years earlier that involved dating violence and how the mother of the female student was unwilling to take the situation seriously when it was reported:

Seven or eight years ago, we had an abusive situation with a couple and they always used to congregate right out here in our rooms and we would see him after school and he would press her up against the windows and he would get in her face and we had to report it obviously. We pulled this girl aside and she was like 'oh, he's fine he'll cool down, he'll cool down,' but you could tell just from the small short interaction that we saw with him that he was doing this all the time to this girl. The counselor called her mom and her mom blew it off too like it was 'Oh well, you know they have their fights.'

Depression, suicidal thought, and the presence of substance abuse were also abundantly witnessed student health-related antecedents to conflict and violence in school. When specifically describing the prevalence within the case environment, Erin stated,

Yeah. I have seen it a lot. I teach mostly all AP US History classes. Advanced placement is a lot work, and most of the kids who are in AP are also in other honors classes, where there is a very heavy workload. There are kids who will joke about, 'Oh, I want to kill myself. Oh, this is so much work. Oh, I want to kill myself,' and sometimes I don't know if they're really joking or not. They post things on Twitter too. They post these meme things that are about giving up and ending it, and 'I have to be perfect, and there's just so much work.'

Betty, who teaches English, described her experiences with both male and female students, in particular when recognizing such emotions within student writing:

> *I feel like it happens so often with kids. Girls will vocalize it more, I think, and guys might talk about it more in their writing. I've had so many students that are male students that described to me that they are depressed, or they're this, and they're that, and they can't let it out at home or they're not supposed to act that way because they're a guy.*

Jasmine described her lack of preparedness in managing depression and suicidal thought among one of her students. Even though Jasmine believed "it's not my job description to deal with that," she still showed concern in dealing with such issues:

> *Eventually this student revealed that she was cutting herself and had all of this stuff. I was just stuck because I didn't know what I should do. Should I council her, or should I give her advice? Because clearly from what she was telling me that was not a good situation for her to be in. But I didn't know what to say. How, as a teacher, do I respond to that? So I felt really unprepared, and I felt like I wasn't helping the student like I should. Even though it's not my job description to deal with that, but when this situation arises, in that state of mind, who knows what that kid could do? And I just felt like I was kind of hopeless and helpless in that.*

Kristen provided insight into how she has dealt with such situations regardless of ones feelings, preparedness, or the veracity of the situation, by stating:

A student who was writing in a notebook, some concerning things in a poem. A lot of it was pretty disturbing. Our counseling staff was wonderful. I set her up immediately with a counselor. We had the mobile crisis team come. I think it's best to err on the side of caution and to teach people that. At least look into it, so that you don't regret not looking into that later.

Teachers also stated that a student's family plays a huge role in the presence of substance abuse as well. For example, Margret stated:

Substance abuse definitely has a presence in the classroom, just because you know it is going on behind closed doors with a lot of these kids. If it's not even necessarily the kids, it's a lot of their parents. That's something too that I've encountered a lot is that a lot of my kids don't live with their parents. They live with a random aunt or an older brother or a grandma because there's a lot of substance abuse issues.

Sally described her frustration with the discipline system regarding the infractions and penalties for student drug possessors. Sally stated, "Here... drug use is a big problem. Sadly, they keep coming back regardless of the seriousness of the infraction." Macy elaborated by stating,

I had a student, it was my first year. Nicest kid and he OD'd on heroin a couple of years ago and I'm seeing it pop up more now. Whether he was addicted while he was here with me, I don't know.

Regarding the presence of an educator's experiences with student-related substance abuse, both assistant administrators agreed that it's a daily problem. Mitch, an assistant administrator, stated that communication must be consistent regarding substance abuse and all of the student health-related topics. He stated,

> *Knowing how to talk within a situation is a huge piece, especially with today's kids. We have more reactive kids because of some of the environments they come from and the age they grew up in. That only inflames the situation. Nine times out of 10.*

Janice, the second assistant administrator, simply stated regarding the presence of substance abuse: "Daily. You're always talking to kids about that kind of stuff." Both assistant administrators stated that they manage every student-health related antecedents to conflict and violence in school on a daily basis, where as teachers exposure to them is present, but more sporadic.

Theme 2: Educators acquire their intervention methods through experience and minimal formal in-service training. Theme 2 was discovered through the answering of interview question 9. This is where the district's required professional development training was first mentioned. The name of this training is called 'Restorative Practices.' This is in-service training for all current educators and new educators to the school district. The training lasts two days, totaling 16 hours. Its purpose is to give all school staff members the opportunities to deescalate a situation between students or between students and staff members if one arises, and to make attempts to lead all parities toward accepting responsibility for their role in the situation. In summary, Restorative Practices involves the use of words and phrases to make a situation calmer. During the interviews, when asked where teachers and administrators currently received their skills to manage such situations involving student-related health issues, Damon stated,

The only training I ever received was when we did our Restorative Practices training, and that's not really about those ideas. It's just…you just figure it out as you go. You know, there are some people in this building that are magnificent at using it, and they use it so well, and you see it work. Then there are other people that kind of use it. I think you have to determine when it's appropriate, like any other set of skills.

Alice described how a "hands on" approach and just getting involved could make a difference. Alice stated,

Hands-on, pretty much. Never really got any specific classes in it. You see two kids about to fight, you step in between them. You try to diffuse the situation. Teach them social skills — it's not acceptable to do this and that. With the depression subject, I'm pretty open with my students. They come to me. I tell them if it's something reportable, I have to report it. I'll tell them, "I think I need to talk to your parents about this. Is that okay?" We have counseling services here that are really good.

Betty agreed by stating she learned through, "Baptism by fire." Jasmine stated, "Well most of it's just from experience, and learning how kids and certain groups of kids work." Kristen agreed by stating, "The skills I have now, I'd say that I probably acquired just over time working with kids."

Restorative Practices was not brought up again until interview questions 11-13.

Theme 3: Educators perceptions vary on their co-workers awareness and management of student health-related issues. Regarding educators views of their fellow co-workers abilities to recognize and appropriately mange conflict, violence, and student's health-related issues, overall the responses were positive and complimentary. However, there were some perspectives that were far less trusting and many teachers were unaware of how their co-workers managed such situations.

On the more positive end, Mary stated:

I think we as a whole, I think we do a really good job here of being pretty cognizant of most of those. Overall I think we do a pretty good job. In an urban school it kind of runs a little bit more above the water sort of thing, whereas I think if you're kind of in a different district then it might get pushed down a little bit more and more masked. I feel like most of the kids kind of wear their hearts on their sleeves here, so we get a general idea of what's going on. As a whole I think we do okay.

Jasmine agreed by stating,

Based on my interactions with them, if something did happen, they would do something. They wouldn't just, you know, brush it off and say, "Oh, whatever, that's not important," because they do all genuinely care about the students.

Margret, while she believed some co-workers handle these situations appropriately, she was less optimistic with others. She stated:

I hate to say it because it sounds a little negative, but I think there is a divide between generations or maybe like newer trained teachers versus older trained teacher. I think when you're working with a population of kids that have the wide variety of issues that our kids do have, you have to exerciser patience. You have to pick your battles sometimes and realize that not every misbehavior in the classroom is really worth fighting a student over. You can hear it in the students too. "Ah, I really like that teacher. She helps me out sometimes. She understands." Or, you hear, "I hate that teacher. He writes me up every time I do this, even if it's like a cell phone out."

Margret also referenced students' perceptions of their teachers in the handling of these situations and their awareness of them, and how this too can influence student's perceptions of their teachers and administrators.

Alice was unaware if her co-workers managed such situations effectively. She stated:

I don't know. I would hope that most of us are aware enough to pick up on those things. I don't know if we're good at it or not. I don't know. It's a hard call.

Erin believed there was a need for more communication. She stated:

I feel that we probably don't talk about it as much as we should as a staff, and that if we see it, we probably should act on it a little more than people currently do, I think.

Betty was less optimistic and believed that some co-workers simply ignore serious situations involving students:

I think it's probably swept under the rug sometimes, because people don't know how to address it, and they think they're going to bring more attention to it and make it a bigger deal than what it is necessarily.

Macy and Damon were the most descriptive with their responses and overwhelmingly believed that their co-workers were unaware of what truly existed in the school building and that their handling of many situations was driven by a lack of trust and feelings of being overwhelmed. Damon stated:

Overwhelmed. They're overwhelmed (teachers and administrators). They don't know what to do. They don't know how to handle it. They are, in many cases, I would just say utterly exhausted.

Macy elaborated by going into the environmental factors that assisted in distrust and an inability for co-workers to manage serious student-related health situations:

A couple years ago we had a whole slew of teachers leave the district. I mean like we like lost 170 teachers in the district a couple of years ago and we were trying to make our voices heard about the administrators handling of discipline and the inconsistencies that occur and to let people know why we were unhappy.

Mitch the assistant administrator was more positive regarding the teacher's management of such situations. He stated:

I think our staff is very good at noticing it and realizing that they can't solve every issue in their classroom. We have teachers that are very quick, and even in our wide range of classroom management, teachers are very quick to recognize, "Hey, something's going on here. I need you to look into this."

However, Janice, the second assistant administrator was not as optimistic. She believed a stronger education and preparation, in particular for newer teachers was necessary. Janice stated:

I think some do. I think some do. However, I think some are very naïve when it comes to stuff. They definitely need some professional development, absolutely to get everybody on the same page of how to properly handle it. Again, going back to some of the younger teachers, they're just trying to survive. Breaking it down with professional development and understanding what world the students are living in and what your role is as a professional when it comes to that stuff, 100 percent.

Many more teachers agreed with Janice, the second assistant administrator, and many were even skeptical of their co-workers abilities to manage and handle situation involving conflict, violence, and student's health-related issues. It was evident that the perceptions of teachers regarding their co-workers ability to manage student related conflict, violence, and the student health-related antecedents to conflict and violence in school, varied. Administrative and teacher distrust also appeared to exist among teachers, administrators and students regarding their ability to follow through with punishments appropriately.

Research Question 3

Individual interview questions 11-13 (Appendix A) aligned with and supported research question 3. These interview questions directly addressed teacher and assistant administrator's current or past perceptions and experiences with in-service education. The interview questions also addressed whether educators believed in-service training appropriately addressed conflict resolution, violence prevention, and the student health-related antecedents to conflict and violent (i.e., bullying, cyber bullying, teenage substance abuse, teenage dating violence, teenage depression and suicidal thought) and what suggestions they had for future training.

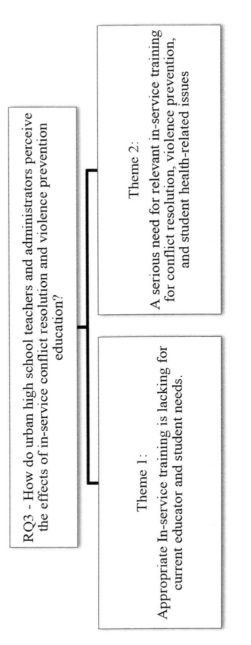

RQ3 - How do urban high school teachers and administrators perceive the effects of in-service conflict resolution and violence prevention education?

Theme 2:
A serious need for relevant in-service training for conflict resolution, violence prevention, and student health-related issues

Theme 1:
Appropriate In-service training is lacking for current educator and student needs.

Figure 3. Themes correlated to Research Question 3.

Theme 1: Appropriate In-service training is lacking for current educator and student needs. When asked about the presence of in-service education, teachers were very forth coming about the times, frequency, and type of such training. Restorative Practices and *ALICE* Training were mentioned, along with professional development for classroom technology use (i.e., Google Classroom). Regarding the presence of mandatory Restorative Practices training for all staff members, teachers believed it to be "ineffective," "corny" and "not relevant to their needs." Damon stated:

> *It's one more thing to do, and it's always the next, best, latest and greatest idea that you never get the chance to perfect before they come up with the next best and "greatest idea." Everybody has a platform. Everyone wants to stand on their soapbox and tell you what they think is best.*

Margret described the differing forms of training they have received by stating:

> *We do a lot of in-service here. So we have daily morning meetings where we kind of do like staff meetings, department meetings, writing tests, blah, blah, blah. As far as like full days in in-service, those are usually curriculum based because right now that's a lot what our district is focusing on.*

Alice elaborated by stating:

> *Yes, we have way too much training. We've got 40 minutes in the morning. It depends on the week. We're supposed to have P.D. (professional development) once a week, 40 minutes. Generally, they pull stuff at the last minute to have*

P.D. on something. It's usually computer-related with Google Classroom, or Google whatever ... everybody had to be trained in Restorative Practice. I do it anyway.

Erin described her training at other schools where she has worked and she expressed her interest in a need for more consistency in a relevant direction. She stated:

I think our school violence trainings focus more on an intruder coming in, or a school shooter. I think that's where most of our school violence focuses on. I've been at three different schools, and at every school I've had to take an online training course that people just breeze through. I think that that's not very helpful. There needs to be more one-on-one, or small-group training on it, and there hasn't really been that kind of stuff at any school I've been at.

Macy described her in-depth perspective of her Restorative Practices training:

Restorative Practices was a complete waste of my life and days that I can never get back. If I've got an issue with a student then I'm confronting the student about it. That's just how I am. Now are there teachers who don't do that? Yes, but Restorative Practices wasn't going to help them to do that. The videos and the trainers that were here, it was all these small little schools and there were elementary kids and there were middle school kids and it was like "you're coming into this school and you have no idea what we're about and you have no idea about the clientele that is at this school." The videos that we watched were all upper elementary school. There was no high school stuff at all.

The assistant administrators were far more trusting of the Restorative Practices methodology and the required in-service training. Mitch stated:

In terms of restorative practice, we are on a cycle for that training. There's a three-day initial course. Then there are refresher courses. There are many positive things that come from this training.

Janice seemed to blame teachers for not accepting the Restorative Practices training:

The common theme among teachers is, "Well, we do that already!" But it provided common language. It provided common language throughout the building for teachers. The people that balk at it are probably the people that need it the most. People said it had no validity "We do it already. I don't need to go through this stuff," well, they were the people that really needed to learn how to develop those relationship pieces in the classroom. I think Restorative Practices have been successful.

However, Mitch did believe that training needed to address teachers concerns and student health-related issues more:

In terms of looking at what other training do we offer outside that… we don't have a ton of refreshers on those things. That's something that maybe we even need to look into. We always are good with our staff meetings and pass along information. If we start to see a trend of increasing, we re-talk about it with the entirety of the staff. In terms of specific questions or means of addressing those kinds of situations, maybe not as much as we should.

Regarding future recommendations for in-service training opportunities and topics to be discussed, teachers and assistant administrators provided many examples. Damon stated:

> *I think that it's such a reactionary approach. It's so reactionary. If you're going to come in to give me PD, I want you to have your pulse on what goes on here, and know that the techniques, the skills. Not "Here's your pamphlet. See you later."*

Margret specified the type of in-service training that was warranted, by stating,

> *We need a more basic understanding of teen psychology and how they perceive the world and issues. I think that would be good. I think just even general PD on teen health and awareness, health type presentations or in-service would be beneficial too.*

Sally suggested:

> *We need professional development to prepare teachers to be able to manage their classrooms in a school setting like ours, in an urban setting would be beneficial. When you're a brand-new teacher; if I came here for my first year I would be really overwhelmed too.*

Betty expressed a serious interest in improving communication during in-service training from the administration towards their teaching staff:

It would be nice to have an administrator that leads small groups that discusses with us, maybe not student names, but what they're seeing in and out of the office on a daily basis, so that we can have more of a concept of what's going on in the building. Don't keep the information hidden from us. We're with students every day after all.

Macy described the lack of communication and the repetitive nature of the current professional development:

They just repeat themselves. I've had like three professional development days this year on the same Google classroom. I'm using Google classroom, I know how to use Google classroom, like put me in something else. Quite frankly the way things are run up at the district office they're just going to fly by the seat of their pants and they're going to come up with something.

Theme 2: A serious need for relevant in-service training for conflict resolution, violence prevention, and student health-related issues. Finally, I had participants answer on a scale of 1 to 10, with 10 being the most important, if they believed formal education on bullying, cyber bullying, teenage dating violence, teenage substance abuse, teenage depression and suicidal thought as antecedents to conflict and violence in school, would benefit the staff and students in this environment. 10 participants stated a score of 10, while four participants stated a score of nine. Shannon adamantly stated,

Most definitely. Most definitely. A 10. Yes. I think we come into our class, and our job is not just teaching anymore. It's a perfect storm for issues going on. Our job is not just teaching.

Margret reiterated the feelings Shannon had by stating,

> *Ten out of ten, for sure because I think especially in this district, again, that is something that we encounter daily in our classrooms. We should want to be aware of these issues and figure out the best ways to deal with them because we deal with them every day anyway. So why not be trained to the best that we can to deal with that kind of stuff.*

Macy appeared to blame higher education and younger generations for the failure of awareness within school environments and the existence of student-related health issues by stating,

> *Absolutely a Ten. It happens every day. Teachers have to deal with this stuff on a daily basis and I don't think that teachers are prepared to deal with that, especially new teachers. I think the educational programs now, because I've had student teachers, I don't think they're getting as much as... there's been a break somewhere. I don't know if it's the generation of these millennials, I don't know what the situation is but I think there's been some breakdown somewhere that I think teachers really need to know what's going on.*

Matt also blamed his lack of undergraduate training for what he is witnessing and is currently experiencing as a classroom teacher:

> *10. 100 percent. You hear more and more stories about kids eight, nine, 10, 12 years old committing suicide over various issues. That's a problem. We need more on, what can we do to prevent it. If we see something, whom do we notify? I think it'd be very useful. I didn't have any of that training in my undergrad.*

Betty drew a link from student wellbeing to academic achievement by stating,

> *Most definitely a 10. I think that it's important. I think that's the most important reason why we're here are the students, and the best way to know them and to meet their needs is to know where they're coming from, being able to identify those things. If they have all those outside factors that they're experiencing, we're not going to get much academically.*

Alice summed up what she believed to be important, and why:

> *Oh, yeah, a 10. I definitely would say that. It's the root of all evil. You can't just heal up here (points to her head). You got to heal the root. Otherwise, it's not going to do any good.*

Both assistant administrators showed an interest in more focused training for the entire staff, specifically regarding the student health-related antecedents to confect and violence in school. Mitch, the first assistant administrator, expressed concern with teachers counseling too much instead of coming to them for help:

> *I would say it would be about a nine. I think it would be just having that knowledge. How to properly, at least, identify it. Do I want teachers counseling on drug addiction? Do I want my teachers doing that? No. I want them to be able to come to us and say, "I need some resources for these kids."*

Janice, the second assistant administrator, pointed to how a lack of knowledge on these issues impacts student success, teacher success, administrator success, and overall school success:

It would be a 10. Again, you're going back to the high-stakes standards as raised test scores, raised test scores, raised test scores. Our kids are not going to invest themselves in the content if all of these other components are knocking at their door or they're not having the focus to do that stuff. Those are real. They exist. If you don't address how to talk kids through those or educate kids on those kinds of things, they're not going to be rock stars in your classroom.

Focus-Group Results

The utilization of focus groups address the research questions being asked (Merriam, 2009). Furthermore, yes or no questions were avoided. Research questions two and three were asked to gain more specificity regarding the case environment. The focus group convened seven days after the initial individual interviews. All 14 participants were invited to the focus group and were reminded of the meeting time and location. However, only eight teacher participants attended. The two assistant administrators were not in attendance, even thought they were apprised of the meeting time and place. The focus group continued with the eight teacher attendees. The focus group lasted less than one hour before regular school hours commenced.

The purpose of the focus group was two fold. First, generated themes from the individual interviews were shared with participants for verification purposes. There were no discrepancies between the generated themes to the research questions and the teacher's beliefs and responses they provided. Second, participating teachers shared experiences involving their interactions with students regarding bullying, cyber bullying, teenage dating violence, teenage substance abuse, teenage depression and suicidal thought, which aligned with research question 2. However, participants had previously shared their experiences regarding research question 2 within the interview phase. Therefore, research question 3 dominated the discussion as participants had little to add regarding research question 2. Attending teachers shared possible topics for future in-service training and professional development for both teachers and administrators, which aligned with research question 3. Responses were audio-recorded, transcribed, coded, and triangulated to the previous interview responses.

When focus group participants were asked about student-to-teacher interactions with bullying, cyber bullying, teenage dating violence, teenage substance abuse, teenage depression and suicidal thought, educators showed a serious interest in what they are legally responsible for, in particular if they witness violent acts outside of the case environment that involve their own students. After triangulating these results from the interview responses of teachers and administrators, new in-service suggestions emerged that had not been previously addressed within the individual interviews. While participants were reluctant to repeat themselves from their previous individual interviews, they did find common ground on the subject of their legal responsibilities when reporting violent acts.

Kristen recalled one incident that involved physical dating violence between a male and a female high school student outside of school:

> *A girl comes into my office and complains that a boy won't stop calling her at home. Mom called the police. Well I saw him yanking her around outside of school I pulled over. At that point I'm thinking to myself, I'm not really sure I should do this. So I'm calling her mom, while calling them over to me. I mean it was bad. People would say we can't do anything for what happens outside of school. I know, but we need to*

do something in case something happens today. Yeah, we may not be able to punish outside, but we have to be able to do something here.

The focus group discussion shifted to discussing in-service opportunities for teachers and parents involving the legal consequences and possible actions that educations can take regarding violence and social media use, in particular outside of school. A recommendation made by three educators stated that outside professional educational legal consolation should occur for school staff, teachers, and administrators. An educational lawyer coming into the school to provide educational law in-service training was overwhelmingly viewed as something that would be beneficial. As focus group participants stated, it's never been previously offered within this case environment. Mary responded to Kristen's situation regarding dating violence, sexual activity, and the legal responsibilities of educators by stating:

We need to teach parents how to work with their kids to make sure they are safe, legally speaking. I don't want to condone it and be like, 'oh yeah they're all going to be doing it so you guys may as well accept it.' They may be doing it, but let's have them at least do it safely. We need this advice regarding how we can or should not intervene.

Macy then commented about the lack of overall education regarding these student health-related antecedents to conflict and violence, in particular dating violence:

No one teaches about the mental and emotional impact of sexual engagement, in particular at a young age. It just turns them and then they go down the road of life just a little off and it changes them without thinking that there is an actual consequence.

Matt then shared his concerns with cyber bullying and how the school staff certainly needs more training on what to do and what they are legally allowed to do:

I think the cyber bullying issue would be good. I think we're aware of it, but what do we do if we see it, really? I think there's a lot of gray area in that concept. Phones are everywhere in this building. I mean, in the hallway, 24/7, a kid's taking a video or a photo, and we might not know it, so how do we deal with that issue, in particular from a legal standpoint?

Regarding the organization of future in-service training, the previous methods the school environment had used were not viewed as favorable among participating teachers. For example, Damon stated,

If you want to actually accomplish something you put a small group, five, 10, whatever individuals in a room and you open a dialogue. And, yes, are there times where there is a staff meeting that has to happen because it's just hard to explain something in an e-mail.

Erin agreed with Damon and also stated that she learns better in small groups, as faculty meetings for important information are typically not taken seriously by staff members:

I think when we get into the whole faculty...people do other things. Nobody's going to full pay attention to the whole thing. I think if it's broken up, then it's a little bit more impactful. I don't think a full group would be beneficial. I don't think anybody would pay attention, or want to be there. If you want to really address these things and face them, then there needs to be more one-on-one, or small-group training on it, and there hasn't really been that kind of focus.

The focus group participants agreed that these were viable solutions to the current state of affairs regarding in-service education within the studied case environment. Participants agreed that in-service training for the student health-related antecedents to conflict and violence in school needed to be formally addressed. Furthermore, the focus group highlighted an interest in educational legal advice for all staff members as a viable in-service opportunity. All members agreed that the results of the focus group and the topics and suggestions discussed throughout should be shared with appropriate school district officials who are responsible for such training (i.e., school level administrators or district officials).

Organizational-Level Logic Model

An organizational-level logic model tracks a chain of events, inputs, and outputs that exist within a specified environment, while looking for consistencies and inconsistencies (Yin, 2009). Logic models also seek to clearly align the vision of an organization based on their perceived goals, current inputs, outputs, and future desired goals (Yin, 2009). The logic model that was generated for this case environment focused on research questions 2 and 3. Within the studied case environment there were three administrative vision statements for the school: (i.e., (a) Student Achievement: Grow all students and maximize individual potential; (b) Staff Growth: Build professional capacity and a culture of collaboration; (c) Community Connections: Engage and communicate with families and community) and required in-service professional development for teachers. However, after analyzing the data, the experiences of both teachers and assistant administrators did not align with either the case-environment's vision statements or the offered in-service training for educators.

Teachers were discouraged with the high frequency, type, and organization of administratively offered in-service education. The experiences of teachers within the case environment were vast, and primarily dealt with the management of student-related bullying, cyber bullying, teenage dating violence, teenage substance abuse, teenage depression and suicidal thought. Teachers suggested new methods for in-service education based on these experiences. These included providing staff with proven scholarly approaches for conflict resolution and violence prevention (i.e., relevant books, research articles), education on the student health-related antecedents to conflict and violence in school, methodologies for information distribution and learning, and in-service level educational legal consultations that would seek to better inform staff members, teachers and administrators. Figure 4 highlights the study results in sequential order including the interview phase, the focus group phase, and the organizational-level logic model.

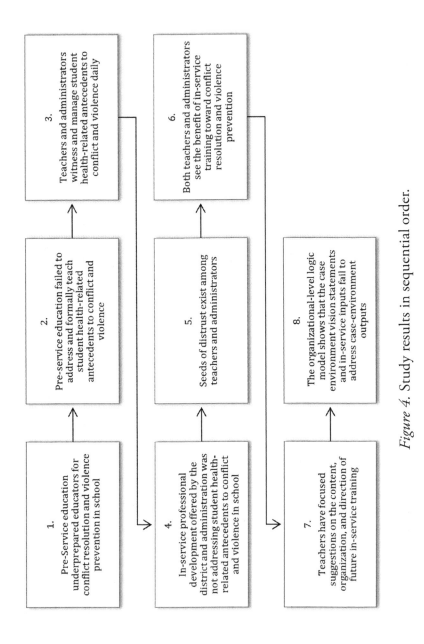

Figure 4. Study results in sequential order.

Summary

The views expressed by participants described the experiences and perceptions of educators' pre-service teacher-education relating to conflict resolution, violence prevention, their interactions with student health-related antecedents to conflict and violence in school, and their perceptions and experiences with in-service education regarding these issues. First and foremost, the results showed that while the pre-service locations of teachers and administrators varied, their lack of exposure to formal education relating to conflict resolution, violence prevention and the student health-related antecedents to conflict and violence in school is overwhelming and abundant. This was true regardless of the teachers or administrators previous pre-service institution, the number of years they've been teaching since they attended undergraduate school, their current grade level taught and their currently taught subject matter.

Secondly, teachers and administrators are exposed to the student health-related antecedents to conflict and violence on a daily basis. Teachers and administrators expressed serious concerns for their students and a serious interest in learning more about these factors. Teachers and administrators believed that this education could be present within pre-service and in-service educator training.

Third, even with the absence of assistant administrators and some teachers within the focus group, the participant's responses verified an interest in more poignant training regarding conflict resolution, violence prevention, and student health-related antecedents to conflict and violence in school. However, the desired in-service training educators were interested in did not include the addition of "programs" or district-wide gimmicks. This also verified the participant's responses from the earlier individual interview phase.

While administrators shared this interest regarding further in-service training within the individual interviews, it appears to be the district officials outside of the case environment that are ultimately responsible for the type, frequency and organization of in-service education. Furthermore, a lack of communication regarding desired in-service education is leading teachers to feel mislead regarding inadequate in-service education, and educators are far less trusting of future in-service training and positive administrative action as a result. In essence, educators know that district officials are also uneducated about conflict and violence in school; therefore they too are also likely to buy into district-wide "prevention programs," games and gimmicks as a false remedy.

The organizational-level logic model also showed an absence of relevant in-service training based on abundant student health-related antecedents to conflict and violence, and the case environments own vision statements. Therefore, the case-environment inputs didn't align with the case-environment outputs. Chapter 5 will discuss an interpretation of the discoveries, along with recommendations for future research. Chapter 5 will also describe the limitations of the investigation and its implications for change, future educational innovation and educational methodology based on the study's theoretical and conceptual frameworks.

DISCUSSION, RECOMMENDATIONS AND CONCLUSIONS REGARDING THE ORIGINS OF SCHOOL VIOLENCE

After exhausting the research throughout the literature review, a clear gap existed regarding the existence of pre-service education for teachers and administrators regarding a formal education on conflict resolution, violence prevention, and the student health-related antecedents that lead to both existing within school-based environments. The key discoveries within this study included:

1. Pre-Service education underprepared educators for conflict resolution and violence prevention in school.

2. Pre-service education failed to address and formally teach student health-related antecedents to conflict and violence.

3. Teachers and administrators witness and manage student health-related antecedents to conflict and violence daily.

4. In-service professional development offered by the district and administration was not addressing student health-related antecedents to conflict and violence in school.

5. Seeds of distrust exist among teachers and administrators.

6. Both teachers and administrators see the benefit of pre-service and in-service training toward conflict resolution and violence prevention.

7. Teachers have focused suggestions on the content, organization, and direction of future in-service training.

8. The organizational-level logic model shows that the school district's vision statements and in-service inputs fail to match existing case-environment outputs.

As varying perceptions of the effectiveness of in-serve training were mentioned throughout the literature review, I began by gathering educator's experiences and perceptions of their pre-service education. Therefore, research findings one and two have a direct impact on the existence of research findings three and four. Research findings five through eight highlighted teachers and administrators perceptions regarding the presence of impactful and relevant in-service training regarding conflict resolution and violence prevention in school. I discovered that many teachers are dedicated to continuous communication involving conflict resolution and violence prevention within the case environment, even with an apparent lack of trust existing at times as highlighted with research finding nine. However, some educators were reluctant to communicate with administration when seeking help, given any perceived distrust.

Within this school district, there were eight elementary schools, two middle schools and one high school. In the previous year before this study was conducted, over 86 teachers quit. The turnover rate for educators and administrators in the K-12 school business is remarkably high. School violence and the frustrations associated with it, are the number one reason why this is the case.

An interpretation of the findings from this research study relating to the conceptual and theoretical frameworks, the literature review, and the participants responses are discussed in this chapter. The limitations, social implications, recommendations for future practices, and future research suggestions based on the current study are also discussed.

Interpretation of Findings

Pre-Service Education

Research question one was based on the lack of evidence and literature discussing the presence of conflict resolution and violence prevention education within pre-service teacher education institutions. As mentioned within Chapter 2, the conceptual framework focused on the (CDC, 2015) Youth Risk Behavior Survey. This survey only previously gathered the perceptions of K-12 students. Therefore, within this study, teachers and administrators were asked about their education relating to five of the 118 health-related antecedents to conflict and violence among students in school.

In total, participants' perceptions of their pre-service under-graduate education came from nine differing undergraduate insti-tutions across six different states in the United States. While some educators within the study discussed being briefly introduced to a student health-related antecedent to conflict and violence within pre-service instruction, participating teachers and administrators described feelings of being overwhelmed and underprepared once they entered their fulltime teaching positions. Teachers and admin-istrators also stated that they largely learned these concepts on the fly, once employed. They firmly believed that an education on stu-dent health-related antecedents to conflict and violence could and should be taught within pre-service teacher education programs.

Both teachers and administrators stated that the absence of these subjects being formally taught within their pre-service in-struction was detrimental to their preparation and it hindered their ability to recognize and manage the occurrences of conflict and violence among students in school. These results confirm the literature within chapter two and the previous studies that indicat-ed how pre-service teachers perceptions vary regarding their per-ceptions of bullying and their abilities to respond to such episodes (Bauman & Del Rio, 2006; Craig, Bell, & Leschied, 2011). The results from this current study also confirmed that the perceptions of educators regarding the presence of school violence preven-tion are needed (Bushman et al., 2016). Therefore, due to edu-cators varying perceptions of the definition of violence, including knowledge of the various forms it can take within school settings (Özabaci & Erkan, 2015), a preparatory education is needed to clearly define these concepts.

The current theoretical framework for this study supports the discoveries of research question one. Past experiences combined with previous knowledge drive educational experiences and how this is dependent on past and current knowledge (Dewey, 1938). Ones understanding of specific areas of study are also driven by our learning experiences (Bandura, 1997). Therefore, if the factors that lead to anger and frustration such as verbal taunts, physical assault, and a lack of social awareness (Agnew, 2001) are not taught, an educators understanding or opportunities for impactful application may not be achieved.

Student Health-Related Antecedents to Conflict and Violence

Research question two addressed the presence of student health-related antecedents to conflict and violence, specifically dealing with the presence of and interactions with bullying, cyber bullying, teenage dating violence, teenage substance abuse, teenage depression and suicidal thought. As mentioned within Chapter two, the conceptual framework focused on the (CDC, 2015) Youth Risk Behavior Survey. Given that the (CDC, 2015) YRBS Report had only been given to K-12 students in the past, I asked educators a modified example regarding their experiences with five student health-related antecedents to conflict and violence. Results indicated that both teachers and administrators confirmed that these student health-related antecedents to conflict and violence in school (i.e., bullying, cyber bullying, teenage dating violence, teenage substance abuse, teenage depression and suicidal thought) are ever-present within the case environment, and the management of such behavior occurs daily.

While teachers mentioned that each student health-related antecedent is abundant and exists within the case environment, their experiences varied on which antecedents to conflict and violence they have personally witnessed. Both administrators immediately stated that they witness and manage each student health-related antecedent to conflict and violence on a daily basis. These findings within the research verify current and past research highlighted within chapter two in that differing perceptions on school-level violence call for further education to deter such acts (Hertzog, Harpel, & Rowley, 2016), Students and school staff members experience many different forms of violence within school environments (Espelage et al., 2013). Furthermore, past research has also concluded that the ability of students to problem solve and resolve conflicts may ultimately be mitigated by the teacher's level of education on such issues (Turkum, 2011). If such an education were present within pre-service education for prospective teachers, an educator's recognition of such issues may allow them to manage and prevent conflict and violence among students.

The discoveries from research question two directly tied into the theoretical framework of this study. Teachers specifically apply meaning through formal education and experiences (Dewey, 1938). If the presence of student health-related antecedents to conflict and violence are not previously or currently taught, educators may not appropriately recognize nor act upon each incident within a school environment. Exposure to such an education could further personal understanding, thereby driving the likelihood of formal action (Bandura, 1977). As one understands that these student health-related factors can lead one toward delinquency and crime (Agnew, 2001), intervention methods may become more frequent. Therefore, the very presence of an education on the student health-related antecedents to conflict and violence in school may help reduce the likelihood of prolonged conflict and violence within school-based environments.

In-Service Education
Research question three directly addressed the perceptions of educators regarding their in-service training toward conflict resolution and violence prevention within their school-based environment.

Teachers believed that their in-service training was not addressing conflict resolution and violence prevention, in particular regarding the student health-related antecedents to conflict and violence. Teachers also stated that past in-service training, in an attempt to address these issues, has fallen short of meeting their needs and was viewed as counterproductive (i.e., Restorative Practices).

The past research within chapter two verified these findings. Bradshaw et al. (2013) argued that teachers were in need of further training regarding student health-related issues. Furthermore, in-service professional development for school violence prevention might also be lacking depending on the previous and current expertise of a school's administration (Charmaraman et al., 2013), as administrators are ultimately responsible for the design of school-based in-service training opportunities. Even though administrators were more optimistic than teachers regarding the current relevance of presently offered in-service training, administrators agreed that in-service training addressing student health-related antecedents to conflict and violence could and should be addressed more frequently and accurately. However, this left teachers feeling less optimistic about the administrator's abilities to address the schools needs and those of the students within in-service education. Furthermore, these perceptions and experiences regarding past and current in-service training generated feelings of distrust between teachers, administrators, and some members of the student population.

These research findings are directly associated with the theoretical framework of general strain theory regarding the removal of positively valued stimuli while presenting a threat to one with noxious or negatively valued stimuli (Agnew, 2006). Previous instruction and personal experiences combined with a continuous understanding of relevant issues for a school environment may lead to relevant and impactful education (Dewey, 1938). However, the quality of those educational experiences (Dewey, 1938) and the overall levels of ones understanding may drive the presence or absence of necessary instruction, thereby shifting the expectations of those we instruct, and ourselves (Bandura, 1997). Any absence of relevant education on conflict and violence in school and the student health-related antecedents that cause both may prolong their existence within a school-based environment.

Focus Group Discoveries

Research question three was the primary question addressed within the focus group. While the results were similar between the interview responses and the focus group responses for this research question, teachers expressed an interest in educational law as a viable option for future in-service training for both themselves and administrators. Teachers expressed this interest in educational legal advice, as such an education has never been offered to them within undergraduate, graduate or in-service instruction. More education regarding the student-health related antecedents to conflict and violence in school were also mentioned as important subjects to be taught within school staff in-service training.

An apparent lack of educational law information and education on the student health-related antecedents to conflict and violence in school appears to be widespread among teachers and administrators. Past research within chapter two aligns with these results. Conflict resolution education is minimal across numerous courses of study within college level instruction for graduate and undergraduate students, including educational law (Zelizer, 2015). Therefore, the efficacy of such subjects may drive the absence of current education or school-level implementation (Bandura, 2016; Schultes, 2014). Any failure to explore needed information to achieve goals may lead to episodes of strain, in particular in educational environments where both adults and youth are present (Agnew, 2006). An education on these two elements that directly contribute to conflict and violence in school may help alleviate current and future problematic episodes. I would also not limit a legal education to only school staff members. The student population should also know their legal rights and what they are legally accountable for.

Organizational-Level Logic Model

Research questions two and three were the primary focus of the organizational-level logic model. This organizational-level logic model highlighted the case environments own vision statements and the presence of their existing in-service training options. These vision statements and in-service education opportunities were compared with what teachers and administrators were experiencing within the case environment. As a result, inconsistences were prevalent throughout, given what in-service training district officials and administrators were offering, and what teachers and administrators were experiencing regarding conflict and violence in school. For example, the presence of technology training was considered redundant and unnecessary among teachers. Therefore, this allotted time for in-service training could be better utilized to educate staff members about the causes of school-related conflict and violence and the student health-related antecedents that contribute to their existence. The presence of Restorative Practices training was also not seen as a viable solution to conflict and violence within a school or classroom setting, yet this training was mandatory for all employees, new employees, and this program was heavily referenced within the case environment.

Teachers and administrators explained throughout the investigation that student health-related antecedents to conflict and violence in school were daily issues. The previously and presently offered in-service training was failing to address any of the student health-related antecedents to conflict and violence in school. Teachers described viable options and potential topics for future in-service training that would address this apparent absence of relevant and applicable in-service education (i.e., educational law and legal responsibilities, bullying, cyber bullying, teenage dating violence, teenage substance abuse, teenage depression and suicidal thought).

Future organizational-level logic models could examine the experiences of students regarding conflict and violence in school. These experiences and perceptions could then be compared to how teachers and administrators are addressing such occurrences to measure consistencies and inconsistencies. Organizational-level logic models could then be shared with stakeholders to properly address continuous improvement within school-based environments.

LIMITATIONS OF THE STUDY

This investigation presented a few limitations worth noting. This research utilized a purposeful sampling of 12 teachers and two assistant administrators. The qualifying participants represented both selection criteria of (1) their geographically diverse pre-service undergraduate teacher-education college or university and (2) their currently taught primary core subject (i.e., math, science, history, and literature), one within each grade level (grades 10-12). In total, nine participants attended differing pre-service undergraduate teacher-education institutions across six different States, while the remaining five participants attended the same pre-service undergraduate teacher-education institution. However, no two participants attended the same institution while achieving the same undergraduate degree. Both assistant administrators attended the same pre-service institution, however, they attended differing graduate degree programs within different states. Three teachers graduated from their pre-service institution without a degree in education, whereas the remaining 11 participants all graduated with an education degree. A possible limitation existed in the participant selection, as all 14 participants did not graduate from 14 differing pre-service colleges or universities. Teachers within the freshman building next to the studied case environment were not selected, nor were exploratory or elective teachers (i.e., those who teach business, physical education, technology). These broader perceptions and experiences could have added to the acquired data.

Some generalizations were made, as many of the case-studied environment's educators attended the same pre-service undergraduate teacher-education university. Therefore, the first preliminary prerequisite for the research was unattainable based on those who volunteered and were willing to participate. However, the second prerequisite was achieved in obtaining the participation of one core-subject teacher from each core subject, within each grade level.

The individual audio-recorded interviews were the primary method of data collection. These interviews heavily relied on participant's abilities to accurately recall past pre-service experiences and their perceptions of that instruction. The participants didn't particularly struggle with their perceptions of past events, as current events within the case environment easily prompted their recollection. The participant's comments did not affect the accuracy of the findings, as even a 30-year veteran of the profession was able to clearly articulate her past pre-service educational experiences.

There were participant limitations within the focus group. While all 14 participants were apprised of the focus group and the meeting time, only eight teachers attended. Four teachers and both assistant administrator were not in attendance. Only one teacher notified me in advance that they would not be in attendance. While limited attendance during the focus group was unexpected, even when numerous advanced prompts were given, administrative input and cross discussion may have allowed for more communication and trust between teachers and administrators regarding current and future in-service training. Possible options of future in-service implementation methods may have been shared by teachers and accepted by administrators in person, thereby potentially increasing the chances of teacher-to-administrator collaboration for future in-service professional development. However, many teachers were not fearful of taking their in-service suggestions to the schools administration, even though administrators were not in attendance for the focus group.

RECOMMENDATIONS

I recommend that future research examine the perceptions of pre-service teacher-education professors at the college and university levels regarding conflict resolution and violence prevention education for prospective teachers. College and university professor's perspectives and past and current knowledge of these relevant issues could be explored. Most of the research within the literature review focused on the existence of student health-related antecedents to conflict and violence in school and the varying perceptions of educators regarding such episodes. Therefore, future studies could highlight school-based environments while assessing which forms of conflict and violence teachers and administrators are experiencing or recognizing. Such measurements may help school-based environments cater their in-service professional development for both teachers and administrators.

Such an education could also be taught to school-aged students. However, health education may be the only school-based subject that covers these topics and this subject may be limited, if not completely absent within in K-12 education. Therefore, its recommended that students within the middle and high-school grade levels receive formal health education on the topics of bullying, cyber bullying, teenage dating violence, teenage substance abuse, teenage depression, suicidal thought and the legal consequences of each, along with many others.

The presence of conflict and violence in school is undeniable. Furthermore, the literature review failed to examine the perceptions of current teachers and administrators regarding their pre-service education programs formally addressing conflict resolution and violence prevention in school. Given these points, a formal education could be in place that addresses such issues before an educator formally enters a school or district as a paid employee. Therefore, I recommended that pre-service teacher education programs at the college and university levels formally teach conflict resolution, violence prevention, and the student health-related antecedents that contribute to their existence within school-based environments. The presence of a formal education at the pre-service level of teacher education may positively impact the quantity and quality of future in-service training regarding conflict resolution and violence prevention in school. A formal education on conflict resolution, violence prevention, and the student health-related antecedents that contribute to their existence, could be accurately addressed within both pre-service and in-service education. The presence of pre-service and in-service training programs addressing these issues may reduce the overall existence of conflict and violence within school-based environments and within individual classrooms.

IMPLICATIONS

The presence of conflict and violence in school impacts both students and educators alike, regardless of the socioeconomic environment (i.e., urban, suburban, rural etc.). The presence of conflict and violence in school also impacts the academic achievement of students and the entire success of the school environment, regardless of the socioeconomic environment. States across the United States of America hold school districts, individual schools, and their educators accountable for student academic achievement and safety. Failing to properly and honestly educate teachers and administrators about conflict resolution, violence prevention, and the student-health related antecedents that contribute to their existence at all levels of formal educator training, is imprudent.

The implications for change directly imply that a formal education on conflict resolution, violence prevention, and the student health-related antecedents that contribute to either are necessary, regardless of the socioeconomic environment one intends to teach in or currently teaches in. Therefore, heightened levels of preparation for teachers and administrators may generate safer school-based environments everywhere. An innovative formal education could begin within pre-service teacher education programs at the college and university levels. This education could continue throughout an educator's in-service training after becoming a paid employee within a school district. Teachers and administrators within school-based environments could seek out viable and appropriate written resources for their staff members to assist in this further education (i.e., peer-reviewed academic articles and books).

With each passing decade, new forms of conflict and violence emerge. These forms of violence also show themselves within school-based practices, classroom and school wide instructional methods, and district school-board level illegality and bureaucratic overreach. As forms of conflict and violence materialize within school-based environments, the necessary education to decrease their existence is failing to follow. Many unproven and falsely believed practices persist, with no knowledge of how such practices are causing the very problems that school-based environments are seeking to eliminate. Pre-service and in-service education that focuses on conflict resolution, violence prevention, student health-related antecedents that contribute to both, and more direct instructional practices that maximize learning and time, rather than wasting it, could alleviate these shortcomings. Furthermore, an accurate assessment of the presence of conflict and violence within all school-based environments could allow school districts and their stakeholders to implement relevant and accurate training opportunities. However, any desired in-service training opportunity should be assessed for its level of effectiveness before implementation occurs.

Figure 5 includes 10 "rabbit holes" which are individually deep, yet interconnected. Each segment, starting with the *Absence of School-Violence Education in Teacher Preparation (Undergraduate/Graduate Instruction)*, individually contains numerous factors that contribute to each highlighted surface-level influence. While these factors may be far too many to list for each highlighted segment, the surface level facts that are shown are enough to paint an objective picture of the school-based landscape and the educational approaches that have led to the existence and perpetuation of violence in school. If the first highlighted segment fails to change in a positive comprehensive direction, nothing within school-based environments will change or improve regarding violence in school.

Figure 5. The origins and root causes of violence in school.

Conclusions

Teachers and administrators are experiencing conflict and violence in school on a daily basis. The absence of formal education within the pre-service and in-service levels of educator training may contribute to the very existence of conflict and violence within school-based environments and its leaving educators who are entering the teaching profession overwhelmed and underprepared.

The findings of this study indicated that undergraduate pre-service teacher education and current in-service training for educators are failing to formally address conflict resolution, violence prevention, and the student health-related antecedents that contribute to conflict and violence in school. This absence of an education exists across numerous pre-service teacher education institutions throughout America. By failing to prepare educators for the inevitability of encountering conflict and violence in school, pre-service teacher education programs may have directly contributed to the previous, current and future existence of conflict and violence within school-based settings. Furthermore, this lack of pre-service formal education on conflict resolution, violence prevention and the student health-related antecedents that contribute to both, are motivating the quality, quantity and relevancy of in-service professional development for current teachers and administrators.

There were numerous serendipitous findings within this study. These findings were not serendipitous in that they impacted the final results, however, they were rather telling and worth repeating as they require further examination within numerous school-based environments. For example, teachers reported that at least one convicted sex offender, who was a 19-year-old high school sophomore student, was allowed to enroll and attend class within this studied school-based environment. This very student also engaged in a sex crime, within the school, against a female teacher. He apparently used a cell phone and recorded this female teacher under her desk as she wore a skirt. Even when caught, the male student was still allowed to attend school. He also returned as a student to that very teacher's classroom for the rest of the year. Not surprisingly and rightfully so, the female teacher quit at years end.

Another finding was the misuse of Twitter by a student who assumed the identity of the school's principal. This student used foul language and racist remarks, along with pictures containing nudity in order to disparage the school's principal. Once caught, the student was suspended, and yet he was still allowed to return to school.

Given the use of Twitter by administrators within school-wide settings to bolster a positive school environment, the administration continued to use Twitter as a means of communication, even after this event caused great embarrassment and professional harm.

A third major finding, and equally as detrimental as the previous two, was an answer by both educators and administrators when I asked them a follow-up question about what books they read in their spare time. Each participant told me that they don't read books about violence in school or educational philosophy, let alone look them up, and that their own district does not provide them such resources. Both teachers and administrators had numerous excuses and reasons for not reading in their spare time, most of which were unfortunately predictable.

Sadly, this continues to be a massive problem within K-12 education. K-12 teachers, administrators, school-board members and superintendents (both local and state level) tend to not read unless they are paid or it's required for advanced certification in some specified area. In my professional opinion, this lack of reading and continuous lack of self-efficacy is a major origin of school-level violence. Or, more nefariously, what if this lack of knowledge of lack or objective resource sharing is being perpetuated on purpose?

School districts need to encourage teachers to access proven scholarly-educational fact regarding these subjects and educators should do this investigation on their own, without prompt. If the cyclical nature of the origins of school violence fail to be broken (Figure 5) and the head of the snake (corruption, illegality, and low self-efficacy within educational environments among adults tasked with protecting minors) is not severed from the body, American school-based education will be fruitless.

Humans make decisions and humans create problems. Problems do not fall from the sky, nor do they appear out of thin air. Sadly, where a human generated problem exists, a human is responsible, and ironically, a subjective opportunist is standing close by ready to provide their "answer" or "solution." Ultimately, this approach is typically delivered through the existence of an additional "prevention program" at a higher cost. These "answers," "solutions" or "prevention programs" that find their way into school-based environments and seek to remedy conflict and violence are not typically grounded in scientific fact, nor do they provide relief in an objective way (i.e., Positive Behavior Interventions and Supports [PBIS], The PAX Good Behavior Game, Restorative Practices, Suspended Curriculum etc.). Those that blind-ly accept outside "prevention programs" tend to be the very groups of people that work hand in hand with those that create them and profit monetarily from their existence. They routinely inhabit the upper echelons of school districts (i.e., influential money lenders, politicians, State-level education officials, school-board members, superintendents etc.). Truth be told, such remedies or programs that are put forth by these individuals or groups, that claim to combat conflict and violence in school, tend to do far more harm than good. This apparent inability to appropriately recognize and prevent the existence of conflict and violence in school, and its real causes, are generating defensiveness, distrust and disillusionment between, among and within school-district employees. This can generate an unhealthy work environment and an unhealthy learn-ing environment for everyone.

Overall, the very structure of school itself and the routines that are forced on students and teachers, which have nothing to do with knowledge acquisition or personal academic evaluation, gen-erate violence within school and among those who inhabit such environments—by default. This is why "prevention programs" are forced on schools instead of books and scientifically reviewed re-search articles (which are also far less expensive). The latter edu-cational experiences and literature undoubtedly prove that school officials, the adults in charge and the policies they create out of thin air, generate and perpetuate the existence of conflict and vio-lence in school—while "prevention programs" blame school-aged students and their families. This is what happens when the un-knowledgeable direct the unknowledgeable—someone might be-lieve something for a lifetime that just isn't true.

Furthermore, it shouldn't be understated that poor classroom instruction is a major, daily antecedent to conflict and violence in school. Students don't need hugs, pampering, competition, games and group work. Grade school students and college students need professionalism, compassion, strong role models, future job training and great instructors who are competent in their subject matter, and the business aspects of the desired future employment options of their students. Any failure to understand the above characteristics of teacher effectiveness will generate the proverbial "slippery slope" that K-12 schools and educators are trying to avoid in the first place.

With all of this stated, one should ask themselves numerous questions given the evidence that has existed throughout history, leading right up to the modern day. For example, is political activism, ideology and indoctrination, which is so readily seen within K-12 schooling and teacher education programs at the undergraduate and graduate levels, a major origin to the existence of violence in school? When pre-service teachers are indoctrinated as undergraduates, are they entering K-12 school systems in America with a level of false ideology that will cost them their employment once it's attained? Are these pre-service teachers not just being set up to fail, but are they being set up to incite division and violence among their students or their fellow staff members?

Furthermore, why aren't students themselves who are violent more than once or twice within K-12 schools permanently removed from school more often, even now with the advent of online home-based K-12 education at their disposal as a logical, healthy alternative? Why are so many "second chances" given to violent offenders within school-based environments, which ultimately makes everyone else unsafe, and this includes adult employees? In the end, I think it's worth asking the ultimate question; with all of this factual scientifically-researched proof available at anyone's fingertips regarding the origins and causes of violence in school, is violence within school-based environments being allowed to happen on purpose? After all, as the saying goes; "The greatest trick the Devil ever pulled was convincing the world he didn't exist." Therefore, in essence, the biggest error an educational institution can make is believing that violence is not a problem or that it doesn't occur where they work, where they live, or that they themselves could ever be responsible for its existence.

In summary, positive change must begin at the undergraduate level of teacher education. In an effort to prepare and educate prospective teachers and administrators for the existence of conflict and violence in school, a formal education addressing these issues should be in place within teacher-education programs. This innovative education should include statistical facts, exposure to historic educational philosophy, scholarly articles and affordable books on related subjects, accompanied by objective curriculum and instructional methods. For example, YouTube videos could frequently be shown that highlight school-based human behaviors and situational scenarios. School-based sociology, adolescent and adult psychology, conflict resolution, violence prevention and the student health-related antecedents that contribute to conflict and violence in school should also be thoroughly investigated. These common sense, relevant and innovative educational approaches could then be applied within in-service training for current educators in order to teach, refresh and remind all of those who work within school-based environments. If such simple, truthful remedies are discouraged, then you may have your answer as to why violence in school exists.

Sadly, but accurately, as Socrates stated, "When you want wisdom and insight as badly as you want to breath, it is then you shall have it." Simply put, don't wait to learn before it's too late.

Epilogue

Upon this study's conclusion, this studied school environment witnessed an investigation of its district superintendent. This superintendent was placed on administrative leave and was ultimately forced to resign as a result of workplace sexual harassment, workplace bullying and intimidation, lying and slanderous practices—among other behaviors that were not specified. He was bought out of his contract and given roughly $225,000 by the district.

At least one female teacher, who was also a coach within the studied high school, was removed from her position and pled guilty to engaging in a felonious sexual relationship with one of her players (a female minor). She received no jail time.

Soon after, a male assistant principal of an elementary school, within the same district, was arrested and fired for possessing crystal meth in his office desk drawer. He was also previously investigated for loaning his car to someone who used it in a robbery, after smoking crystal meth with him first. This assistant principal was charged with felonious drug possession, is currently facing possible jail time of 180 days as a maximum sentence, and his educator's license was permanently revoked.

All of these above offenders were Caucasian. Students also brought guns and knives to school and death threats were made to others over social media. All of these stories made the local televised news, online news outlets and local newspapers.

Appendix A

Interview Questions

One-on-One Formal Interview Questions for Teachers and Administrators

Preliminary Interview Questions:

Name
Age
Gender
Number of years taught
Subject taught
Grade levels taught
Locations taught
Name and location of pre-service teacher education institution
Year you graduated from college
Highest degree attained
Name and location of Graduate Institution/if applicable

Pre-service/Past:

1. What do you remember as the <u>primary emphasis</u> of your pre-service teacher education coursework/program?

2. Reflecting on your pre-service program was there a <u>specific course dedicated</u> to the topic of school violence and conflict resolution? *If the answer is "no", then you move on to the next question#3. If the answer is "yes" then you ask the following question.*

   2.1 Would you describe the content of the course?

3. Reflecting on your pre-service experience, were there any <u>specific events or workshops,</u> independent of your coursework, dedicated to the topic of school violence and conflict resolution?

   If the answer is "no" then you move on to the next question #4. If "yes", then ask the following question.

   3.1 Would you describe these events or workshops?

4. Which of the following topics were included in your pre-service program?
   a. bullying
   b. cyber bullying
   c. dating violence
   d. substance abuse
   e. depression and suicidal thought

   If the answer is "no" then move on to question #5. If "yes", then ask the following question.

4.1 Describe what you remember about the following topics.
   a.   bullying
   b.   cyber bullying
   c.   dating violence
   d.   substance abuse
   e.   depression and suicidal thought

5. Were any of the following topics <u>included in any component of your graduate</u> coursework or program?
   a.   bullying
   b.   cyber bullying
   c.   dating violence
   d.   substance abuse
   e.   depression and suicidal thought

If the answer is "no" then you move on to question #6. If "yes", then ask the following question.

5.1 Describe what you remember about the following
   a.   bullying
   b.   cyber bullying
   c.   dating violence
   d.   substance abuse
   e.   depression and suicidal thought

6. Do you remember any episodes during <u>student teaching</u> where you felt particularly prepared or unprepared to respond to episodes of:
   a.   bullying
   b.   cyber bullying

    c.   dating violence

    d.   substance abuse

    e.   depression and suicidal thought

7. Do you have any <u>recommendations</u> on how pre-service or graduate teacher education programs might better prepare students for conflict resolution and violence prevention capacity in schools?

Student to Teacher Interactions:

8. Would you <u>describe any experiences</u> that you have had with students on the topics of:

    a.   bullying

    b.   cyber bullying

    c.   dating violence

    d.   substance abuse

    e.   depression and suicidal thought

9. Where did you acquire your current skills to <u>intervene</u> in student episodes of

    a.   bullying

    b.   cyber bullying

    c.   dating violence

    d.   substance abuse

    e.   depression and suicidal thought

10. What are your thoughts the following topics <u>being recognized</u> among your co-workers:

    a.   bullying

    b.   cyber bullying

c. dating violence
d. substance abuse
e. depression and suicidal thought

In-service/Current:

11. Do you currently have in-service training for teachers?

    11.1 How often does it take place?

    11.2 What topics have been addressed?

    11.3 How successful do you feel the in-services have been?

12. Do you have any suggestions on in-service professional development programs that might better prepare their teachers and administrators to respond conflict resolution and violence prevention in school?

13. On a scale of 1 to 10, with 10 being the most important, do you believe formal education on bullying, cyber bullying, depression, dating violence, or substance abuse, and suicidal thoughts as antecedents to conflict and violence in school would benefit the staff and students in this environment?

Rating ( )

    13.1 Why have you assigned this question that number?

REFERENCES

Abbott, C. H., & Zakriski, A. L. (2014). Grief and Attitudes Toward Suicide in Peers Affected by a Cluster of Suicides as Adolescents. *Suicide & Life-Threatening Behavior, 44*(6), 668-681. doi:10.1111/sltb.12100

Agnew, R. (2001). Building on the foundation of general strain theory: Specifying the types of strain most likely to lead to crime and delinquency. *Journal of Research In Crime And Delinquency, 38*(4), 319-361. doi:10.1177/0022427801038004001

Agnew, R. (2006). *Pressured into Crime: An Overview of General Strain Theory.* Los Angeles, CA: Roxbury.

Agnich, L. E., & Miyazaki, Y. (2013). A Multilevel Cross-National Analysis of Direct and Indirect Forms of School Violence. *Journal of School Violence, 12*(4), 319-339.

Aricak, O. T., & Ozbay, A. (2016). Investigation of the relationship between cyber-bullying, cybervictimization, alexithymia and anger expression styles among adolescents. *Computers In Human Behavior, 55*(Part A), 278-285. doi:10.1016/j.chb.2015.09.015

Baldry, A. C., Farrington, D. P., & Sorrentino, A. (2016). Cyber-bullying in youth: A pattern of disruptive behavior. *Psicologia Educativa, 22*(1), 19-26. doi:10.1016/j.pse.2016.02.001

Bandura, A. (1977). Self-efficacy: Toward a unifying theory of behavioral change. *Psychological Review, 84*(2), 191-215. doi:10.1037/0033-295X.84.2.191

Bandura, A. (1997). *Self-efficacy: The exercise of control.* New York: Freeman.

Bandura, A. (2016). Moral disengagement: How people do harm and live with themselves. New York: Worth Publishers.

Bauman, S., & Del Rio, A. (2006). Pre-service teachers' responses to bullying scenarios. Comparing physical, verbal, and relational bullying. *Journal of Educational Psychology, 98*, 219-231.

Bavarian, N., Duncan, R., Lewis, K. M., Miao, A., & Washburn, I. J. (2015). Adolescent Substance Use Following Participation in a Universal Drug Prevention Program: Examining Relationships With Program Recall and Baseline Use Status. *Substance Abuse, 36*(3), 359-367. doi:10.1080/08897077.2014.952364

Bell, K. S., & Willis, W. G. (2016). Teachers' perceptions of bullying among youth. *Journal of Educational Research, 109*(2), 159-168. doi:10.1080/00220671.2014.931833).

Blair, R. R. (2010). Psychopathy, frustration, and reactive aggression: the role of ventromedial prefrontal cortex. *British Journal of Psychology (London, England: 1953), 101*(Pt 3), 383-399. doi:10.1348/000712609X418480

Bonell, C., Wells, H., Harden, A., Jamal, F., Fletcher, A., Thomas, J., & Moore, L. (2013). The effects on student health of interventions modifying the school environment: systematic review. *Journal of Epidemiology & Community Health*, *67*(8), 677-681. doi:10.1136/jech-2012-202247

Bourke, L., Humphreys, J., & Lukaitis, F. (2009). Health behaviors of young, rural residents: A case study. *Australian Journal of Rural Health*, *17*(2), 86-91. doi:10.1111/j.1440-1584.2008.01022.x

Bradshaw, C. P., Waasdorp, T. E., O'Brennan, L. M., & Gulemetova, M. (2013). Teachers' and education support professionals' perspectives on bullying and prevention: Findings from a national education association study. *School psychology review*, *42*(3), 280.

Bushman, B. J., Newman, K., Calvert, S. L., Downey, G., Dredze, M., Gottfredson, M., & Webster, D. W. (2016). Youth violence: What we know and what we need to know. *The American Psychologist*, *71*(1), 17-39. doi:10.1037/a0039687

Centers for Disease Control and Prevention, (2015). Youth Risk Behavior Surveillance System. National Youth Risk Behavior Survey Overview (YRBS). Retrieved from: http://www.cdc.gov/yrbs/. Accessed on 2016.

Charmaraman, L., Jones, A. E., Stein, N., & Espelage, D. L. (2013). Is It Bullying or Sexual Harassment? Knowledge, Attitudes, and Professional Development Experiences of Middle School Staff. *Journal of School Health*, *83*(6), 438-444. doi:10.1111/josh.12048

Chronister, K. M., Marsiglio, M. C., Linville, D., & Lantrip, K. R. (2014). The Influence of Dating Violence on Adolescent Girls' Educational Experiences. *Counseling Psychologist, 42*(3), 374-405. doi:10.1177/0011000012470569

Cochran-Smith, M. (2006): 'Policy, Practice, and Politics in Teacher Education', Thousand Oaks, CA: Corwin Press

Coker, A. L., Clear, E. R., Garcia, L. S., Asaolu, I. O., Cook-Craig, P. G., Brancato, C. J., & ... Fisher, B. S. (2014). Dating Violence Victimization and Perpetration Rates Among High School Students. *Violence Against Women, 20*(10), 1220-1238. doi:10.1177/1077801214551289

Coles, M. E., Ravid, A., Gibb, B., George-Denn, D., Bronstein, L. R., & McLeod, S. (2016). Adolescent mental health literacy: Young people's knowledge of depression and social anxiety disorder. *Journal of Adolescent Health, 58*(1), 57-62. doi:10.1016/j.jadohealth.2015.09.017

Craig, K., Bell, D., & Leschied, A. (2011). Pre-service teachers' knowledge and attitudes regarding school-based bullying. *Canadian Journal of Education, 34*(2), 21-33.

Creamer, M. R., Portillo, G. V., Clendennen, S. L., & Perry, C. L. (2016). Is Adolescent Poly-tobacco Use Associated with Alcohol and Other Drug Use?. *American Journal of Health Behavior, 40*(1), 117-122. doi:10.5993/AJHB.40.1.13

Crepeau-Hobson, F., & Leech, N. L. (2016). Peer Victimization and Suicidal Behaviors Among High School Youth. *Journal of School Violence, 15*(3), 302-321. doi:10.1080/15388220. 2014.996717

Cuadrado-Gordillo, I., & Fernández-Antelo, I. (2016). Adolescents' perception of the characterizing dimensions of cyber-bullying: Differentiation between bullies' and victims' perceptions. *Computers In Human Behavior*, *55*(Part B), 653-663. doi:10.1016/j.chb.2015.10.005

Dahlberg, L.L, & Krug, E.G. (2002). Violence: a global public health problem. In: Krug EG, Dahlberg LL, Mercy JA, Zwi AB, Lozano R, editors. World report on violence and health. Geneva (Switzerland): World Health Organization; 2002. p. 1-21.

David-Ferdon, C., Simon, T. R., & National Center for Injury Prevention and Control (DHHS/CDC), D. P. (2014). Preventing Youth Violence: Opportunities for Action.

Debnam, K. J., Johnson, S. L., & Bradshaw, C. P. (2014). Examining the Association Between Bullying and Adolescent Concerns About Teen Dating Violence. *Journal of School Health*, *84*(7), 421-428. doi:10.1111/josh.12170

DeCamp, W., & Bakken, N. W. (2016). Self-injury, suicide ideation, and sexual orientation: differences in causes and correlates among high school students. *Journal of Injury & Violence Research*, *8*(1), 15-24. doi:10.5249/jivr.v8i1.545

Dewey, J. (1938). *Experience and education*. New York: MacMillan.

Di Bona, V. L., & Erausquin, J. T. (2014). Drug Use Risk Behavior Co-Occurrence Among United States High School Students. *Journal of Child & Adolescent Substance Abuse*, *23*(2), 87-90. doi:10.1080/1067828X.2012.748596

Dooley, J. J., Shaw, T., & Cross, D. (2012). The association between the mental health and behavioral problems of students and their reactions to cyber-victimization. *The European Journal of Developmental Psychology*, 9(2), 275–289. http://dx.doi.org/10. 1080/17405629.2011.648425.

Duggins, S. D., Kuperminc, G. P., Henrich, C. C., Smalls-Glover, C., & Perilla, J. L. (2016). Aggression among adolescent victims of school bullying: Protective roles of family and school connectedness. *Psychology of Violence*, 6(2), 205-212. doi:10.1037/a0039439

Dunne, M., Sabates, R., Bosumtwi-Sam, C., & Owusu, A. (2013). Peer Relations, Violence and School Attendance: Analyses of Bullying in Senior High Schools in Ghana. *Journal of Development Studies*, 49(2), 285-300. doi:10.1080/00220388.201 2.671472

Eom, E., Restaino, S., Perkins, A. M., Neveln, N., & Harrington, J. W. (2015). Sexual Harassment in Middle and High School Children and Effects on Physical and Mental Health. *Clinical Pediatrics*, 54(5), 430-438 9p. doi:10.1177/0009922814553430

Erreygers, S., Pabian, S., Vandebosch, H., & Baillien, E. (2016). Helping behavior among adolescent bystanders of cyber-bullying: The role of impulsivity. *Learning And Individual Differences*, 4861-67. doi:10.1016/j.lindif.2016.03.003

Espelage, D. L., Polanin, J. R., & Low, S. K. (2014). Teacher and staff perceptions of school environment as predictors of student aggression, victimization, and willingness to intervene in bullying situations. *School Psychology Quarterly, 29*(3), 287-305. doi:10.1037/spq0000072

Espelage, D., Anderman, E. M., Brown, V. E., Jones, A., Lane, K. L., McMahon, S. D., & ... Reynolds, C. R. (2013). Understanding and preventing violence directed against teachers: Recommendations for a national research, practice, and policy agenda. *American Psychologist, 68*(2), 75-87. doi:10.1037/a0031307

Espil, F. M., Viana, A. G., & Dixon, L. J. (2016). Post-traumatic Stress Disorder and Depressive Symptoms Among Inpatient Adolescents: The Underlying Role of Emotion Regulation. *Residential Treatment For Children & Youth, 33*(1), 51-68. doi:10.1080/0886571X.2016.1159939

Evans, R., & Hurrell, C. (2016). The role of schools in children and young people's self-harm and suicide: systematic review and meta-ethnography of qualitative research. *BMC Public Health, 16*1-16. doi:10.1186/s12889-016-3065-2

Fahy, A. E., Stansfeld, S. A., Smuk, M., Smith, N. R., Cummins, S., & Clark, C. (2016). Longitudinal associations between cyber-bullying involvement and adolescent mental health. *Journal of Adolescent Health*, doi:10.1016/j.jadohealth.2016.06.006

Feldman, M. A., Ojanen, T., Gesten, E. L., Smith-Schrandt, H., Brannick, M., Totura, C. W., & ... Brown, K. (2014). The effects of middle school bullying and victimization on adjustment through high school: growth modeling of achievement, school attendance, and disciplinary trajectories. *Psychology In The Schools, 51*(10), 1046-1062. doi:10.1002/pits.21799

Fletcher, A., Fitzgerald-Yau, N., Jones, R., Allen, E., Viner, R. M., & Bonell, C. (2014). Brief re- port: Cyber-bullying perpetration and its associations with socio-demographics, aggressive behavior at school, and mental health outcomes. Journal of Adolescence, 37(8), 1393–1398. http://dx.doi.org/10.1016/j.adolescence.2014.10.005.

Forsyth, Donelson R. (2009). *Group Dynamics* (5th ed.). Boston, MA: Wadsworth Cengage Learning.

Gavine, A. J., Donnelly, P. D., & Williams, D. J. (2016). Effectiveness of universal school-based programs for prevention of violence in adolescents. *Psychology Of Violence*, 6(3), 390-399. doi:10.1037/vio0000052

Giordano, P. C., Kaufman, A. M., Manning, W. D., & Longmore, M. A. (2015). Teen Dating Violence: The Influence of Friendships and School Context. *Sociological Focus*, 48(2), 150-171. doi:10.1080/00380237.2015.1007024

Gome-Garibello, C., Sayka, C., Moore, K., & Talwar, V. (2013). Educators' Ability to Detect True and False Bullying Statements. *Educational Research Quarterly*, 37(1), 3-23.

Guimond, F., Brendgen, M., Vitaro, F., Dionne, G., & Boivin, M. (2015). Peer Victimization and Anxiety in Genetically Vulnerable Youth: The Protective Roles of Teachers' Self-Efficacy and Anti-Bullying Classroom Rules. *Journal of Abnormal Child Psychology*, 43(6), 1095-1106. doi:10.1007/s10802-015-0001-3

Gumpel, T. P. (2016). Prolonged Stress, PTSD, and Depression Among School Aggressors and Victims. *Journal of Aggression,*

Maltreatment & Trauma, 25(2), 180-196. doi:10.1080/1092 6771.2015.1107169

Hamer den, A. H., & Konijn, E. A. (2016). Can emotion regulation serve as a tool in combating cyber-bullying?. *Personality And Individual Differences, 102*1-6. doi:10.1016/j. paid.2016.06.033

Hamer den, A., Konijn, E. A., & Keijer, M. G. (2014). Cyber-bullying behavior and adolescents' use of media with antisocial content: a cyclic process model. *Cyberpsychology, Behavior And Social Networking, 17*(2), 74-81. doi:10.1089/ cyber.2012.0307

Hecker, T., Hermenau, K., Salmen, C., Teicher, M., & Elbert, T. (2016). Harsh discipline relates to internalizing problems and cognitive functioning: findings from a cross-sectional study with school children in Tanzania. *BMC Psychiatry, 161*-9. doi:10.1186/s12888-016-0828-3

Herrera, J., Kupczynski, L., & Mundy, M. (2015). The Impact of Training on Faculty and Student Perceptions of Cyber-bullying in an Urban South Central Texas Middle School. *Research In Higher Education Journal, 27*

Hertzog, J. L., Harpel, T., & Rowley, R. (2016). Is It Bullying, Teen Dating Violence, or Both? Student, School Staff, and Parent Perceptions. *Children & Schools, 38*(1), 21-29. doi:10.1093/ cs/cdv037

Hildenbrand, A. K., Daly, B. P., Nicholls, E., Brooks-Holliday, S., & Kloss, J. D. (2013). Increased Risk for School Violence-Related Behaviors Among Adolescents With Insufficient Sleep.

Journal of School Health, *83*(6), 408-414. doi:10.1111/josh.12044

Hinduja, S., & Patchin, J. W. (2007). Offline consequences of online victimization: School violence and delinquency. *Journal of School Violence*, 6(3), 89–112. http://dx.doi.org/ 10.1300/J202v06n03_06.

Horan, S. M., Chory, R. M., Carton, S. T., Miller, E., & Raposo, P. J. (2013). Testing Leader–Member Exchange Theory as a Lens to Understand Students' Classroom Justice Perceptions and Antisocial Communication. *Communication Quarterly*, *61*(5), 497-518. doi:10.1080/01463373.2013.799511

Indoshi, F. C. (2003). Teachers' Experiences of the Probation Period of Teaching in Kenya: implications for teacher induction policies and programs. *Journal of In-service Education*, *29*(3), 473-488.

James, K., Bunch, J., & Clay-Warner, J. (2015). Perceived injustice and school violence: An application of general strain theory. *Youth Violence And Juvenile Justice*, *13*(2), 169-189. doi:10.1177/1541204014521251

Jesús Gázquez, J., del Carmen Pérez-Fuentes, M., del Mar Molero, M., Barragán Martín, A. B., Marios Martínez, A., & Sánchez-Marchán, C. (2016). Drug use in adolescents in relation to social support and reactive and proactive aggressive behavior. *Psicothema*, *28*(3), 318-322. doi:10.7334/psicothema2015.327

Jouriles, E. N., Rosenfield, D., Yule, K., Sargent, K. S., & McDonald, R. (2016). Predicting High-School Students' Bystander Behavior in Simulated Dating Violence Situations.

Journal of Adolescent Health, 58(3), 345-351. doi:10.1016/j. jadohealth.2015.11.009

Jun Sung, H., Jungup, L., Espelage, D. L., Hunter, S. C., Patton, D. U., Rivers, T., & ... Rivers, T. J. (2016). Understanding the Correlates of Face-to-Face and Cyber-bullying Victimization Among U.S. Adolescents: A Social-Ecological Analysis. *Violence & Victims, 31*(4), 638-663. doi:10.1891/0886-6708. VV-D-15-00014

Kelly, A. B., Chan, G. K., Mason, W. A., & Williams, J. W. (2015). The relationship between psychological distress and adolescent polydrug use. *Psychology of Addictive Behaviors, 29*(3), 787-793. doi:10.1037/adb0000068

Kelly, A. B., Evans-Whipp, T. J., Smith, R., Chan, G. K., Toumbourou, J. W., Patton, G. C., & ... Catalano, R. F. (2015). A longitudinal study of the association of adolescent polydrug use, alcohol use and high school non-completion. *Addiction, 110*(4), 627-635. doi:10.1111/add.12829

Kikas, E., & Timoštšuk, I. (2016). Student teachers' knowledge about children with ADHD and depression and its relations to emotions. *Emotional & Behavioral Difficulties, 21*(2), 190-204. doi:10.1080/13632752.2015.1069086

Kolbert, J. B., Crothers, L. M., Bundick, M. J., Wells, D. S., Buzgon, J., Berbary, C., & ... Senko, K. (2015). Teachers' Perceptions of Bullying of Lesbian, Gay, Bisexual, Transgender, and Questioning (LGBTQ) Students in a Southwestern Pennsylvania Sample. *Behavioral Sciences (2076-328X), 5*(2), 247-263. doi:10.3390/bs5020247

Kranzler, A., Young, J. F., Hankin, B. L., Abela, J. Z., Elias, M. J., & Selby, E. A. (2016). Emotional Awareness: A Transdiagnostic Predictor of Depression and Anxiety for Children and Adolescents. *Journal of Clinical Child & Adolescent Psychology*, *45*(3), 262-269. doi:10.1080/15374416.2014.987379

Lai, E. Y., Kwok, C., Wong, P. C., Fu, K., Law, Y., & Yip, P. F. (2016). The Effectiveness and Sustainability of a Universal School-Based Program for Preventing Depression in Chinese Adolescents: A Follow-Up Study Using Quasi-Experimental Design. *Plos ONE*, *11*(2), 1-20. doi:10.1371/journal.pone.0149854

Lee, J., Tice, K., Collins, D., Brown, A., Smith, C., & Fox, J. (2012). Assessing Student Teaching Experiences: Teacher Candidates' Perceptions of Preparedness. *Educational Research Quarterly*, *36*(2), 3-20.

Levesque, R. J. R. (2012). Impulsivity. In R. J. R. Levesque (Ed.), Encyclopedia of adolescence. 1. (pp. 1399–1401). Springer Science & Business Media.

Li, K., Simons-Morton, B., Gee, B., & Hingson, R. (2016). Marijuana-, alcohol-, and drug-impaired driving among emerging adults: Changes from high school to one-year post-high school. *Journal of Safety Research*, 5815-20. doi:10.1016/j.jsr.2016.05.003

Long, M. (2016). Aggression and Risky Behaviors in High School Students: An Examination of Bullying. *Nursing Research*, *65*(2), E18.

Lormand, D. K., Markham, C. M., Peskin, M. F., Byrd, T. L., Addy, R. C., Baumler, E., & Tortolero, S. R. (2013). Dating

Violence among Urban, Minority, Middle School Youth and Associated Sexual Risk Behaviors and Substance Use. *Journal of School Health*, *83*(6), 415-421.

Lucas-Molina, B., Williamson, A. A., Pulido, R., & Pérez-Albéniz, A. (2015). Effects of Teacher-Student Relationships on Peer Harassment: A Multilevel Study. *Psychology In The Schools*, *52*(3), 298-315.

Lundgren, R., & Amin, A. (2015). Addressing intimate partner violence and sexual violence among adolescents: Emerging evidence of effectiveness. *Journal of Adolescent Health*, *56*(1, Suppl), S42-S50. doi:10.1016/j.jadohealth.2014.08.012

Marsh, L., McGee, R., & Williams, S. (2014). School Climate and Aggression among New Zealand High School Students. *New Zealand Journal of Psychology*, *43*(1), 28-37.

Matoti, S. N., & Lekhu, M. A. (2016). Sources of anxiety among pre-service teachers on field placement experience. *Journal of Psychology In Africa*, *26*(3), 304-307. doi:10.1080/14330237 .2016.1185921

Mehdinezhad, V., & Mansouri, M. (2016). School Principals' Leadership Behaviors and Its Relation with Teachers' Sense of Self-Efficacy. *International Journal of Instruction*, *9*(2), 51-60.

Melkevik, O., Hauge, L. J., Bendtsen, P., Reneflot, A., Mykletun, A., & Aarø, L. E. (2016). Associations between delayed completion of high school and educational attainment and symptom levels of anxiety and depression in adulthood. *BMC Psychiatry*, *16*1-7. doi:10.1186/s12888-016-0765-1

Mercado-Crespo, M. C., & Mbah, A. K. (2013). Race and ethnicity, substance use, and physical aggression among U.S. high school students. *Journal of Interpersonal Violence, 28*(7), 1367-1384. doi:10.1177/0886260512468234

Merriam, Sharan B. (2009) *Qualitative Research: a guide to design and implementation* San Francisco, Calif.: Jossey-Bass.

Monks, C. P., Mahdavi, J., & Rix, K. (2016). The emergence of cyber-bullying in childhood: Parent and teacher perspectives. *Psicologia Educativa, 22*(1), 39-48. doi:10.1016/j.pse.2016.02.002

Mueller, A. S., James, W., Abrutyn, S., & Levin, M. L. (2015). Suicide ideation and bullying among US adolescents: examining the intersections of sexual orientation, gender, and race/ethnicity. *American Journal of Public Health, 105*(5), 980-985. doi:10.2105/AJPH.2014.3023916

Nahapetyan, L., Orpinas, P., Song, X., & Holland, K. (2014). Longitudinal Association of Suicidal Ideation and Physical Dating Violence among High School Students. *Journal of Youth & Adolescence, 43*(4), 629-640. doi:10.1007/s10964-013-0006-

Nicholson, M. (1992). *Rationality and the Analysis of International Conflict*. Cambridge University Press. p. 11.

Niolon, P. H., Vivolo-Kantor, A. M., Latzman, N. E., Valle, L. A., Kuoh, H., Burton, T., & ... Tharp, A. T. (2015). Prevalence of teen dating violence and co-occurring risk factors among middle school youth in high-risk urban communities. *Journal of Adolescent Health, 56*(2, Suppl 2), S5-S13. doi:10.1016/j.jadohealth.2014.07.019

Obermaier, M., Fawzi, N., & Koch, T. (2016). Bystanding or standing by? How the number of bystanders affects the intention to intervene in cyber-bullying. *New Media & Society*, *18*(8), 1491-1507. doi:10.1177/1461444814563519

Onrust, S. A., Otten, R., Lammers, J., & Smit, F. (2016). School-based programs to reduce and prevent substance use in different age groups: What works for whom? Systematic review and meta-regression analysis. *Clinical Psychology Review*, *44*45-59. doi:10.1016/j.cpr.2015.11.002

Orpinas, P., Nahapetyan, L., Song, X., McNicholas, C. and Reeves, P. M. (2012), Psychological Dating Violence Perpetration and Victimization: Trajectories From Middle to High School. *Aggressive Behavior*, 38: 510–520. doi:10.1002/ab.21441

Özabaci, N., & Erkan, Z. (2015). Metaphors about Violence by Pre-Service Teachers. *Collegium Antropologicum*, *39*(1), 193-201.

Palamar, J. (2014). Predictors of Disapproval toward 'Hard Drug' Use among High School Seniors in the US. *Prevention Science*, *15*(5), 725-735. doi:10.1007/s11121-013-0436-0

Palamar, J. J., Fenstermaker, M., Kamboukos, D., Ompad, D. C., Cleland, C. M., & Weitzman, M. (2014). Adverse psychosocial outcomes associated with drug use among US high school seniors: a comparison of alcohol and marijuana. *American Journal of Drug & Alcohol Abuse*, *40*(6), 438-446. doi:10.3109/00952990.2014.943371

Park-Higgerson, H., Perumean-Chaney, S., Bartolucci, A., Grimley, D., & Singh, K. (2008). The evaluation of school-based violence prevention programs: a meta-analysis. *Jour-*

nal of School Health, *78*(9), 465-479. doi:10.1111/j.1746-1561.2008.00332.x

Parker, E. M., & Bradshaw, C. P. (2015). Teen dating violence victimization and patterns of substance use among high school students. *Journal of Adolescent Health, 57*(4), 441-447. doi:10.1016/j.jadohealth.2015.06.013

Perkins, H. W., Perkins, J. M., & Craig, D. W. (2014). No Safe Haven: Locations of Harassment and Bullying Victimization in Middle Schools. *Journal of School Health, 84*(12), 810-818 9p. doi:10.1111/josh.12208

Peurača, B., & Vejmelka, L. (2015). Non-violent Conflict Resolution in Peer Interactions: Croatian Experience of Peer Mediation in Schools. *Social Work Review / Revista De Asistenta Sociala, 14*(4), 123-143.

Powers, J. D., Wegmann, K., Blackman, K., & Swick, D. C. (2014). Increasing awareness of child mental health issues among elementary school staff. *Families In Society, 95*(1), 43-50. doi:10.1606/1044-3894.2014.95.6

Ribeiro, I. M. P., Ribeiro, Á. S. T., Pratesi, R., & Gandolfi, L. (2015). Prevalence of various forms of violence among school students/Prevalência das várias formas de violência entre escolares. *Acta Paulista De Enfermagem, 28*(1), 54-59.

Rice, E., Petering, R., Rhoades, H., Winetrobe, H., Goldbach, J., Plant, A., & ... Kordic, T. (2015). Cyber-bullying Perpetration and Victimization Among Middle-School Students. *American Journal of Public Health, 105*(3), e66-e72. doi:10.2105/AJPH.2014.302393

Richard, J. F., Schneider, B. H., & Mallet, P. (2012). Revisiting the whole-school approach to bullying: Really looking at the whole school. *School Psychology International*, *33*(3), 263-284.

Romera, E. M., Cano, J., García-Fernández, C., & Ortega-Ruiz, R. (2016). Cyber-bullying: Social Competence, Motivation and Peer Relationships. *Comunicar*, *24*(48), 71-79. doi:10.3916/C48-2016-07

Rothman, E. F., & Xuan, Z. (2014). Trends in physical dating violence victimization among U.S. High school students, 1999–2011. *Journal of School Violence*, *13*(3), 277-290. doi:10.1080/15388220.2013.847377

Sari, S. V. (2016). Was it just joke? Cyber-bullying perpetrations and their styles of humor. *Computers In Human Behavior*, *54*555-559. doi:10.1016/j.chb.2015.08.053

Schultes, M.-T., Stefanek, E., Van de Schoot, R., Strohmeier, D., & Spiel, C. (2014). Measuring Implementation of a School-Based Violence Prevention Program: Fidelity and Teachers' Responsiveness as Predictors of Proximal Outcomes. *Zeitschrift für Psychologie*, *222*(1), 49–57. doi:10.1027/2151-2604/a000165

Shim, H., & Shin, E. (2016). Peer-group pressure as a moderator of the relationship between attitude toward cyber-bullying and cyber-bullying behaviors on mobile instant messengers. *Telematics & Informatics*, *33*(1), 17-24. doi:10.1016/j.tele.2015.06.002

Shorey, R., Fite, P., Choi, H., Cohen, J., Stuart, G., Temple, J., & ... Temple, J. R. (2015). Dating Violence and Substance Use as Longitudinal Predictors of Adolescents' Risky Sexual

Behavior. *Prevention Science, 16*(6), 853-861. doi:10.1007/s11121-015-0556-9

Singsuriya, P. (2016). Conflict resolution, logic of identity and recognition through narrative. *Global Change, Peace & Security, 28*(2), 197-212. doi:10.1080/14781158.2016.1158158

Stake, R. E. (1978). The case study method in social inquiry. *Educational researcher, 7*(2), 5-8.

Stake, R. E. (1995). The art of case study research. Thousand Oaks: Sage Publications.

Suldo, S. M., Gelley, C. D., Roth, R. A., & Bateman, L. P. (2015). Influence of peer social experiences on positive and negative indicators of mental health among high school students. *Psychology In The Schools, 52*(5), 431-446. doi:10.1002/pits.21834

Tobin, K., Ritchie, S., Oakley, J., Mergard, V., & Hudson, P. (2013). Relationships between emotional climate and the fluency of classroom interactions. *Learning Environments Research, 16*(1), 71-89. doi:10.1007/s10984-013-9125-y

Tsang, S. K., Hui, E., & Law, B. C. (2012). Bystander position-taking in school bullying: The role of positive identity, self-efficacy and self-determination. *International Journal of Child Health & Human Development, 5*(1), 103-110.

Tsorbatzoudis, H., Travlos, A. K., & Rodafinos, A. (2013). Gender and age differences in self-reported aggression of high school students. *Journal of Interpersonal Violence, 28*(8), 1709-1725. doi:10.1177/0886260512468323

Ttofi, M. M., Farrington, D. P., Lösel, F., Crago, R. V., & Theodorakis, N. (2016). School bullying and drug use later in life: A meta-analytic investigation. *School Psychology Quarterly*, *31*(1), 8-27. doi:10.1037/spq0000120

Tucker, J. S., Troxel, W. M., Ewing, B. A., D'Amico, E. J., & D'Amico, E. J. (2016). Alcohol mixed with energy drinks: Associations with risky drinking and functioning in high school. *Drug & Alcohol Dependence*, *167*36-41. doi:10.1016/j.drugalcdep.2016.07.016

Türküm, A.S., 2011. Social Supports Preferred by the Teachers when Facing School

Violence. *Children and Youth Services Review.* Vol. 33 (5), pp.644-650.

Vagi, K. J., O'Malley Olsen, E., Basile, K. C., & Vivolo-Kantor, A. M. (2015). Teen Dating Violence (Physical and Sexual) Among US High School Students: Findings From the 2013 National Youth Risk Behavior Survey. *JAMA Pediatrics*, *169*(5), 474-482. doi:10.1001/jamapediatrics.2014.3577

Valdebenito, S., Ttofi, M., & Eisner, M. (2015). Prevalence rates of drug use among school bullies and victims: A systematic review and meta-analysis of cross-sectional studies. *Aggression & Violent Behavior*, *23*137-146. doi:10.1016/j.avb.2015.05.004

Van Nuland, S. (2011). Teacher education in Canada. Journal of Education for Teaching, Volume 37 (4). DOI: 10.1080/02607476.2011.611222

Washburn, I. J., & Capaldi, D. M. (2014). Influences on Boys' Marijuana Use in High School: A Two-Part Random Intercept Growth Model. *Journal of Research On Adolescence (Wiley-Blackwell)*, *24*(1), 117-130. doi:10.1111/jora.12030

Wiederhold, B. K. (2014). Cyber-bullying and LGBTQ youth: a deadly combination. *Cyberpsychology, Behavior And Social Networking*, *17*(9), 569-570. doi:10.1089/cyber.2014.1521

Williams, J., Miller, S., Cutbush, S., Gibbs, D., Clinton-Sherrod, M., & Jones, S. (2015). A latent transition model of the effects of a teen dating violence prevention initiative. *Journal of Adolescent Health*, *56*(2, Suppl 2), S27-S32. doi:10.1016/j.jadohealth.2014.08.019

Willits, D., Broidy, L. M., & Denman, K. (2015). Schools and Drug Markets: Examining the Relationship between Schools and Neighborhood Drug Crime. *Youth & Society*, *47*(5), 634-658.

World Health Organization. (2017). Adolescents: health risks and solutions (Fact sheet 345). Retrieved from http://www.who.int/mediacentre/factsheets/fs345/en/

Yin, R. K. (2009). Case study research: Design and methods (4th ed.). Thousand Oaks, CA: Sage.

Yu, C., Li, X., Wang, S., & Zhang, W. (2016). Teacher autonomy support reduces adolescent anxiety and depression: An 18-month longitudinal study. *Journal of Adolescence*, *49*115-123. doi:10.1016/j.adolescence.2016.03.001

Zelizer, C. (2015). The role of conflict resolution graduate education in training the next generation of practitioners and scholars. *Peace And Conflict: Journal of Peace Psychology*, *21*(4), 589-603. doi:10.1037/pac0000135

About the Author

Dr. Sean M. Brooks earned a B.S. in Health Education, an M.S. in Education with a specialization in technology integration in the classroom, and a Ph.D. in Education with a specialization in learning, instruction and innovation.

Dr. Brooks was a public-school teacher, grades 6-12, for nine years. He has spoken nationally and internationally on the topics of conflict and violence in school, prevention techniques, teacher education, teacher leadership, curriculum, instruction and classroom management.

Dr. Brooks is the author of the books; *Where The Finger Points, Violence Among Students and School Staff: Understanding and Preventing the Causes of School Violence,* and *The Mental and Emotional State of School-Aged Students: What Exists and What Educators Can Do.*